# GHOST TOWNS
## of CALIFORNIA

Your Guide to the Hidden History and
Old West Haunts of California

Philip Varney

Voyageur Press

First published in 2012 by Voyageur Press, an imprint of MBI Publishing Company and the Quayside Publishing Group,
400 First Avenue North, Suite 300, Minneapolis, MN 55401 USA

Voyageur Press titles are also available at discounts in bulk quantity for industrial or sales-promotional use. For details write to
Special Sales Manager at Quayside Publishing Group, 400 First Avenue North, Suite 300, Minneapolis, MN 55401 USA.

To find out more about our books, visit us online at www.voyageurpress.com.

ISBN-13: 978-0-7603-4082-0

Library of Congress Cataloging-in-Publication Data

Varney, Philip.
 Ghost towns of California : your guide to the hidden history and Old West haunts of California / text and photography by Philip Varney.
   p. cm.
 Includes bibliographical references and index.
 Summary: "A guide to the best ghost towns of California. Once thriving, these abandoned mining camps and pioneer villages still ring with
history. Philip Varney equips you with everything you need to explore these sites, including maps, directions, history, and photos"--Provided
by publisher.
 ISBN 978-0-7603-4082-0
 1. Ghost towns--California--History. 2. California--History, Local. 3. Mining camps--California--History. 4. Frontier and pioneer life--California.
 5. California--Guidebooks. I. Title.
 F869.A15V37 2012
 979.4--dc23
                     2012004810

Editor: Adam Brunner
Design Manager: Cindy Samargia Laun
Cartographer: Patti Isaacs, Parrot Graphics
Book designer: Mandy Kimlinger

Printed in China

10 9 8 7 6 5 4 3 2 1

**Front cover main:** Bodie's Main Street.
**Front cover bottom left:** Bodie's Boone Store and Warehouse.
**Front cover bottom right:** James B. Perry headstone, Bodie cemetery.
**Back cover top left:** Ryan's recreation hall and movie theatre.
**Back cover top right:** Interior of the Coloma schoolhouse.
**Back cover bottom:** A restored trestle at the Kentucky Mine, Sierra City.
**Page 1:** The Bodie townsite.
**Page 2:** A crumbling trestle in Cerro Gordo. *Photograph by Michael Moore*
**Page 3:** The interior of Bodie's Boone Store and Warehouse.
**Opposite page:** A beautiful view of the Sierra Nevada from Cerro Gordo. *Photograph by Michael Moore*

**FOR WARREN WEAVER**
AND
**IN MEMORY OF MARY SHUMWAY WEAVER**

# CONTENTS

# TO THE READER

*Ghost Towns of California* is intended for people who seek the unusual, enjoy history, and savor solitude. Some of the destinations in this book will be unfamiliar even to most Californians, like out-of-the-way Campo Seco, Goffs, and Helena. Other sites attract thousands of visitors annually, such as Columbia, Bodie, and Calico. Chasing down the ghost towns and mining camps in this book will take you from sea level to elevations exceeding 8,000 feet. You will view some of the West's loveliest rivers, driest deserts, and grandest mountaintops. In the process, I hope you will see California as you have never seen it before. That certainly happened to me.

I was a ghost town hunter long before I became a ghost town writer. I have been prowling California's back roads in search of the forgotten since 1974. My third ghost town book, published in 1990, covered California from the Mexican border to Death Valley and Inyo County. My sixth ghost town book, published in 2001, extended north from New Idria, in the hills southwest of Fresno, through the '49er Gold Rush Country, made a surprising stop in San Francisco Bay, and proceeded to the northern and eastern reaches of California.

The book you have in your hands takes the best towns from those two books and adds sites I overlooked in those volumes. All entries have been revised, in some cases extensively, from their original versions. As a prime example, in my Southern California book, Death Valley's Ryan received only passing attention because it was closed to the public and could only be photographed from a distance. This book features the first authorized published photos of Ryan since the 1930s, and I provide an extensive description of what remains at Ryan today. The site is still closed to the public, at this writing, but I was given special permission to visit, photograph, and even stay for several nights.

If you want to find more sites than I have featured here, those two recommended books are listed under my name in the bibliography at the end of this book.

I wrote my first book, *Arizona's Best Ghost Towns*, as a result of my frustration with the way other such books generally had been organized: Most of them had the ghost towns listed alphabetically, not organized geographically, which seemed far more logical to me. Some books had their maps buried in the back instead of

The City Hotel in Columbia offers only the finest amenities.

up with the ghost towns themselves. I wanted a completely practical, informative guide that would give me everything I needed next to me on the seat of my truck. That first book's success led to seven more.

This volume, like my other books, arranges towns so you can visit places in natural groups, beginning with Coloma, where the Gold Rush began, and ending with Llano, an abandoned ghost of the Mojave Desert.

Each chapter features a map of the area, a history of each town, specific directions to each site, and recommendations when necessary for vehicle requirements. For example, some towns are on paved roads near major highways, while others are on dirt roads and require a high-clearance vehicle. Although I never needed to use four-wheel drive for this book, I did utilize it on recent visits to two sites, Cerro Gordo and Leadfield. I have also accessed each of these sites in a two-wheel drive pickup.

You might be interested to know, for this book, how I selected which towns to include and which to exclude. To begin, if there is very little left at a site, it's not going to be included unless it is in proximity to another, better site. For example, although Kelso offers only one major historic building (a *very good* historic building, however), it is along the route between two worthy sites, Shoshone and Calico.

At the other end of the spectrum are former ghost town sites that have been thrust into the twenty-first century. Visitors to Gold Rush Country may wonder why I have not included some important towns along Highway 49, like Auburn, Placerville, and Sonora, all of which were definitely historically significant. Quite simply, if a town seemed "buried under modernity," as author-historian Richard Dillon put it, I omitted it. For example, although Placerville has some lovely downtown buildings, the twentieth and twenty-first centuries have rather overwhelmed the nineteenth.

A person new to ghost town hunting might tour the second entry in this book, Georgetown, and wonder just what I consider a ghost town to be, because Georgetown has shops, restaurants, a hotel, and an elegant bed and breakfast inn. In addition, its population more than triples on occasional festive weekends. By my definition, a ghost town has two characteristics: the population has decreased markedly, and the initial reason for its settlement (such as mining) no longer keeps people there. At the peak of its mining frenzy, Georgetown had an estimated population of well over 10,000 citizens; as of the 2010 census, 2,367 people live there, and virtually no one makes a living in a mine. A ghost town, then, can be completely deserted, like Skidoo, Helena, and Llano; it can have a few residents,

Ruins in Campo Seco.

like Chinese Camp, Shoshone, and Willow Springs; it can be protected for posterity by the State of California, like Coloma, Columbia, and Bodie; or it can have genuine signs of vitality, like Murphys, Downieville, and Weaverville. But in each case, the town is a shadow of its former self.

I had mixed feelings about charming, smaller towns like Sutter Creek and Jamestown. They weren't quite so obviously up-to-date, and both feature attractive business districts and residences, but they still seemed on the whole to be too, well, *bustling* for my taste. Since you will be traveling through many of these towns on your way to others, feel free to explore them on your own.

I also omitted many towns that I have enjoyed visiting but felt that the buildings weren't sufficiently distinct architecturally. These towns were the most difficult to exclude, because virtually all ghost towns are interesting at some level. So, to fans of Hornitos, Sheep Ranch, and Gold Run, all I can say is that I had to eliminate towns, and these were some of the last to go. I was standing in each of them when I made my decision.

One site not included in this revision, I am sad to say, is the aforementioned town of New Idria, because thirteen of its buildings were destroyed by a suspected arsonist in 2010, leaving precious little to see.

People living in sleepy places like Dutch Flat, Locke, and Keeler may be offended about inclusion in a "ghost town" book. But their communities have "ghost town" indicators: in each case, their population has dropped precipitously, and once-bustling businesses and schools have closed.

Some guide books I have used when traveling in the West were apparently written principally for armchair travelers. Unfortunately, some have been written by armchair authors. I cringe when I realize that a book I'm using has been written by someone who obviously hasn't personally observed what he is writing about. I first saw some of the sites in this book in the late 1970s and early 1980s. But I visited or revisited every single site in 2010 and 2011. The photographs in this book were all taken within that same time period. The book's emphasis is on what remains at a town, not what was there in its heyday. I describe what to look for at each site, and I suggest walking and driving tours.

TO THE READER

The Murphys Hotel at night.

I also make recommendations about museums, mine tours, and mill tours. To see them all would be expensive and somewhat repetitious, so I give advice based on comparisons to similar tours throughout the West. My observations are candid, and I received no special consideration at such sites. I paid all entrance fees at attractions, and guides knew me only as another tourist.

Speaking of being just another tourist, I received no special access to sites for photography other than at Ryan, in Death Valley. For previous books, my photographer partners, John and Susan Drew, and I paid for permits or were given special privileges because of the projects. I did not do that for this volume. I also put away all my film cameras and lenses and, for the first time, used a digital camera with only two zoom lenses. I did not use either a flash or a tripod. I wanted to take photos that any person could take. If you like the photos of interiors in North Bloomfield or Bodie, you can take the same shots through a window, just as I did. I enlisted the help of my good friend, Dr. Michael Moore, who is an accomplished photographer and my mentor when it comes to digital photography. I also invited him to submit images for Chapters 5 and 6, and seven of his photographs were selected.

When it comes to looking for photographic subjects, I suggest starting with graveyards. Almost every town has a cemetery, even if it has little else. Some of my most enjoyable but poignant moments have come while walking around graveyards, since emotions are often laid bare on tombstones. To read the grief of parents in the epitaphs of their children is to see the West in absolutely personal terms. History comes tragically alive in cemeteries, and headstones make wonderful photographic subjects, as you will see in this book.

To visit all of the sites in this book without frantically racing from one to another, I would estimate that you would need from three weeks to a month. You might plan for a bit longer just to allow for other attractions you might find along the way—and weather. I took months more than that and drove thousands of miles farther than you will, but then I was looking at many ghost towns that I eliminated. I also needed to photograph in optimum light, so seeing a wonderful, photogenic place like Bodie at noon was not acceptable.

Why are we called to these places where so many lives have toiled and so many have been forgotten? My late friend, mystery writer Tony Hillerman, in a foreword to my book *New Mexico's Best Ghost Towns*, captured the answer:

"To me, to many of my friends, to scores of thousands of Americans, these ghost towns offer a sort of touching-place with the past. We stand in their dust and try to project our imagination backward into what they were long ago. Now and then, if the mood and the light and the weather are exactly right, we almost succeed."

Our "touching-places with the past," however, are in immediate and long-term danger. Vandals tear up floorboards hoping for a nonexistent coin. Looters remove an old door with the vague notion of using it, only to discard it later. Thieves dislodge a child's headstone, heartlessly assuming no one will miss it.

Remember: These old towns are to be explored and photographed, but also protected and treasured. You must be a part of the preservation, not the destruction. As you visit the places in this book, please remember that ghost towns are extremely fragile. Leave a site as you found it. I have seen many items on the back roads that tempted me, but I have no collection of artifacts. If you must pick up something, how about a fast food wrapper or a soft drink can?

When I was doing fieldwork for my book *Ghost Towns of Colorado*, I found the following notice posted in a lovely but deteriorating house. It eloquently conveys what our deportment should be at ghost towns and historic spots:

Attention: We hope that you are enjoying looking at our heritage. The structure may last many more years for others to see and enjoy if everyone like you treads lightly and takes only memories and pictures.

—*Philip Varney*
*Tucson*

**Important Note**: *The State of California has, at this writing, slated many California State Parks for closure beginning in 2012 for budgetary reasons. Five of the sites in this book (North Bloomfield and the Malakoff Diggins, Plumas-Eureka, Shasta, the Weaverville Joss House, and China Camp) are state parks or contain state parks within them. Be certain that the places you want to visit are open. See the individual entries in the text; in each case I give my assessment of how seriously that closing will affect your enjoyment of the site in question. The easiest way to check is to go to http://www.parks.ca.gov. One of the subheadings will be "park closures."*

# INTRODUCTION
## GOLD! GOLD! GOLD FROM THE AMERICAN RIVER!

When James Marshall found gold in California's American River on January 24, 1848, he set into motion one of the most incredible economic and social upheavals in history. When he made his find, California was still a part of Mexico. Nine days later, Mexico ceded to the United States a vast territory west from Texas and north to Oregon. In doing so, Mexico gave up, unknowingly, the most astonishing concentration of gold the world has ever seen.

Originally Marshall's find was viewed with skepticism. A San Francisco newspaper in May of 1848 scoffed, "A few fools have hurried to the [American River], but you may be sure there is nothing in it."

A few days later, however, storekeeper Sam Brannan, who had been to the area of Marshall's discovery, paraded through San Francisco with a bottle full of gold dust, exclaiming, "Gold! Gold! Gold from the American River!" The rush was on, and San Francisco practically emptied, its citizens heading to the gold fields—and conveniently passing Brannan's store, full of supplies, along the way (Brannan would become one of California's wealthiest men and reportedly its first millionaire). Another of the city's newspapers complained a few days later that "the field is left half planted, the house half built, and everything neglected but the manufacture of shovels and pick axes." San Francisco's harbor eventually was clogged with rotting, crewless ships.

In the year of 1848, only 400 people immigrated to California. During the following year, with word of Marshall's discovery trumpeted across the nation, and then the world, an astounding 90,000 people descended upon the area. Author J. S. Holliday states that California "would be transformed from obscurity to world prominence; . . . from a society of neighbors and families to one of strangers and transients; from an ox-cart economy based on hides and tallow to a complex economy based on gold mining."

Gold seekers swarmed from across the nation on the early pioneer trails that had opened the West, like the Oregon and Santa Fe trails. Some attempted short cuts across infamous Death Valley, while others took a southern route that

*A wooden headstone in Bodie.*

crossed arid sections of Arizona and Mexico. The average successful trip took about a hundred days and covered two thousand miles.

Those who could afford the passage often opted for sea travel. A 15,000-mile journey from New York to San Francisco around Cape Horn took from five to eight months, but those willing to brave the dangers of the jungle could cross the isthmus in Nicaragua or Panama and shorten the sea voyage to six or eight weeks.

Whatever route they used, the Argonauts came and came. Between 1848 and 1860, California's population exploded from 14,000 to 300,000. In the early days of the rush, the population was almost exclusively male. One lad in Nevada City inscribed in his diary, "Got nearer to a female this evening than I have been for six months. Came near fainting."

Not all the hopefuls came from the United States, although estimates start at more than sixty-five percent American. Mexicans and Chileans streamed in from the south. English, Scots, Irish, and Welsh, many of them experienced miners, came from the British Isles. Germans, French, and Scandinavians arrived. By 1852, about 25,000 Chinese had joined the throng, looking for the promised wealth of *Gum Shan*, "The Golden Mountain."

The reason for the stampede was genuine. The Mother Lode was an immense body of gold that extended down the western foothills of the Sierra Nevada (Spanish for "snow-covered range") for an unbelievable distance of a hundred miles. It began north of Coloma and ended near Bear Valley (an area covered in Chapter 1 of this book).

Although the Mother Lode was the most famous, other extremely rich deposits were found in Nevada, Placer, and Sierra Counties (Chapter 2). A third bonanza was revealed only two months after Marshall's discovery when Major Pierson B. Reading found gold more than 200 miles north of San Francisco, leading to a separate gold rush near the Trinity and Klamath Rivers (Chapter 3). The size and scope of the California Gold Rush defies simple description, but it can be capsulated in two almost unimaginable facts: in a mere four years, the world's supply of gold *doubled*, and with the United States leading the way, more gold was discovered worldwide between 1850 and 1875 than in the previous 350 years combined.

Initially, gold was easily retrieved from secondary deposits in streams and along banks. The gold's size varied from small particles, known as "flour gold," to nuggets weighing as much as several pounds. Prospectors would then search upstream for the source of that water-borne gold. Those primary deposits were often so pure that gold could be extracted with a shovel—or even a spoon.

A recurring pattern developed in the quest for riches. As Henry David Thoreau said of the Argonauts, "They go to dig where they never planted, to reap where they never sowed." Prospectors were exploring everywhere that looked promising. When a discovery was made, there would be a futile attempt at secrecy. After the revelation, there would be a frantic dash to stake claims—or jump someone else's. Frequently, once the word was out, the discovery would be wildly exaggerated. Mark Twain, who witnessed the Gold Rush firsthand, once defined a mine as "a hole in the ground owned by a liar."

The Boone Store and Warehouse in Bodie holds a true mystery: A safe stands inside that no one can open, and no one knows what is inside.

At the site of each new bonanza, a tent city appeared. If the deposits lasted, more permanent wooden buildings would be constructed, bringing merchants, saloonkeepers, prostitutes, and eventually a postmaster. Everyone in camp depended upon gold in one way or another. Some camps turned into full-fledged towns with solid brick buildings and signs of gentility, like newspapers and an opera house. When the gold deposits failed, however, the town would empty and the same cycle would begin anew at the next "El Dorado."

The easy pickings of the Gold Rush were exhausted by the 1860s. Getting to the more difficult deposits required hard-rock quartz mining and, later, newer methods—hydraulicking and dredging. These procedures required capital investment, elaborate equipment, and an organized workforce, basically ending the era of the single miner working his small claim.

Even large-scale mining eventually gave out, although some mines produced for decades after the Gold Rush bonanza ended around 1884.

Inventions in the industrialized world had an enormous effect upon the United States, nowhere more dramatically than in California. Vastly improved communication came with Samuel Morse's improved electromagnetic telegraph in 1832 and Alexander Graham Bell's patenting of the telephone in 1876. Mining gained a powerful force for moving earth with the invention of dynamite in 1867 by Swedish chemist Alfred Nobel.

But nothing changed the American West—and California—as much as the completion of the First Transcontinental Railroad in 1869. The British publication

*The Economist*, in the middle of the nineteenth century, commented that in the 1820s the speed a man could go unaided was about four miles per hour, "the same as Adam." By horse, it was up to about ten miles per hour for any distance. But, *The Economist* went on, by the 1850s, a man could, by train, habitually go forty miles per hour and occasionally as high as *seventy*.

The transcontinental railroad linked the Midwest to California. The journey that Argonauts took in 1849 to the Gold Rush, which, as previously mentioned, took an average of about a hundred days, was reduced only twenty years later to *seven* days. Stagecoach lines became obsolete. The Oregon Trail, one of the original routes—using one branch or another—to the Mother Lode, became a relic. And the effect upon mining was enormous: with railroads to carry ore out and supplies in, costs were significantly decreased. Ore that had previously been too expensive to mine, mill, and smelt could now yield a healthy profit. Mines that had been abandoned were reopened and mined profitably, and their tailings were reprocessed for overlooked gold, using new technology. (Note: For the definition of mining terms like "lode" and "Argonaut," consult the glossary on pages 229–231.)

Nevertheless, mining towns are created to fail, as they exist to extract a finite quantity. When that quantity is gone, the town is doomed—unless it can find another way to prosper.

Many of the towns in the first three chapters of this book did indeed find a new way to prosper by becoming charming places people want to visit. But the others have faded almost to obscurity.

The last four chapters of this book leave Gold Rush Country. Not all mining in California was for gold, and not all ghost towns were once mining camps. Several unusual and interesting sites stand not far from the Mother Lode near San Francisco Bay (Chapter 4).

During the decline of Mother Lode mining, a new strike in the 1870s brought a short but glorious life to the now-spectacular ghost town of Bodie, east of the Sierra Nevada (Chapter 5). South of Bodie in the same chapter stand several more ghost towns east of the Sierras well worth exploring, including Cerro Gordo, the first site in this book that was rich in silver, not gold. Cerro Gordo, improbable as it may seem, helped to turn Los Angeles from a sleepy pueblo into a major metropolis.

Prospectors learned to endure many hardships in their quest for riches. Nowhere is that more evident than in the final two chapters of this book. Death

Valley (Chapter 6), where untold numbers of prospectors died from the harsh elements, produced modest yields of gold, silver, and lead, but the real bonanza there was found in a more mundane commodity—borax. As the world discovered its many uses, borax became by far the most profitable mineral extricated from Death Valley.

The Mojave Desert (Chapter 7) also created challenges for miners, railroad builders, farmers, ranchers, and travelers who simply wanted to cross it. The enticement of mineral riches brought hardy people to the landscape in spite of the dangers, and when huge gold deposits were found in Randsburg, along with silver and borax in Calico, the rush was on yet again.

To experience California's mining history, one can explore its remnants: the mining camps and ghost towns that were eventually abandoned in search of new wealth. The tent camps have disappeared. Visitors can walk empty hillsides where a thousand people once lived and not see a trace of their presence. The majority of wood-frame towns have vanished as well, having fallen to fire, vandalism, salvage, or the most final of all forces—gravity. Some delightful ones still exist, however, and the best are showcased throughout this book.

The communities with brick buildings, as one might expect, have generally survived the best. Chapter 1's Columbia, for example, is an historic treasure. Most, however, have become the "old town" sections of modern cities that rather overwhelm their historic districts.

That does not mean, however, that no true exploits await the reader who follows the back roads of this book: there is nothing for the ghost town enthusiast that rivals the thrill of entering a tiny and charming town like North Bloomfield or exploring the brick ruins of Shasta. Often the adventure is enhanced by the journey itself, like ascending the Yellow Grade Road to Cerro Gordo or heading into stunning Titus Canyon beyond Leadfield. Sometimes the excitement is the inherent solitude of many sites, like somnolent China Camp or Campo Seco. And even in the very-much-alive towns, like Murphys and Nevada City, an invigorating energy and sense of history surrounds you as you stroll with shoppers who have visited nearby wineries and have spent the night at delightful bed and breakfast inns. Finally, there is nothing quite as contemplative as a visit to a ghost town cemetery, where many unanswered mysteries are posed on the half-told tales of headstones.

Your California ghost town adventure begins here.

# 1

# GHOSTS
## OF THE
# MOTHER
# LODE

THE CALIFORNIA GOLD RUSH CHANGED THE COURSE OF HUMAN HISTORY, not just in the United States, but also across the globe. People worldwide, hoping for a markedly better life, abandoned their situations and headed for California. The population of California exploded from about 26,000 to more than 380,000 in only twelve years, with a large percentage of that number descending upon the sites in this chapter along with many other towns that have either become major communities or have disappeared completely.

The historic towns of the Mother Lode vary from busy small cities like Placerville and Jackson to two state parks, Coloma and Columbia, and to charming, picturesque communities like Georgetown, Volcano, Amador City, Mokelumne Hill, and Murphys. Even with all the gift shops, wineries, bed and breakfast inns, and historic hotels, there is still room in the Mother Lode for two real ghost towns: Campo Seco and Chinese Camp.

James Marshall's statue points dramatically down to the spot on the American River where Marshall first saw gold.

Across the street from the Saint Charles Saloon in Columbia.

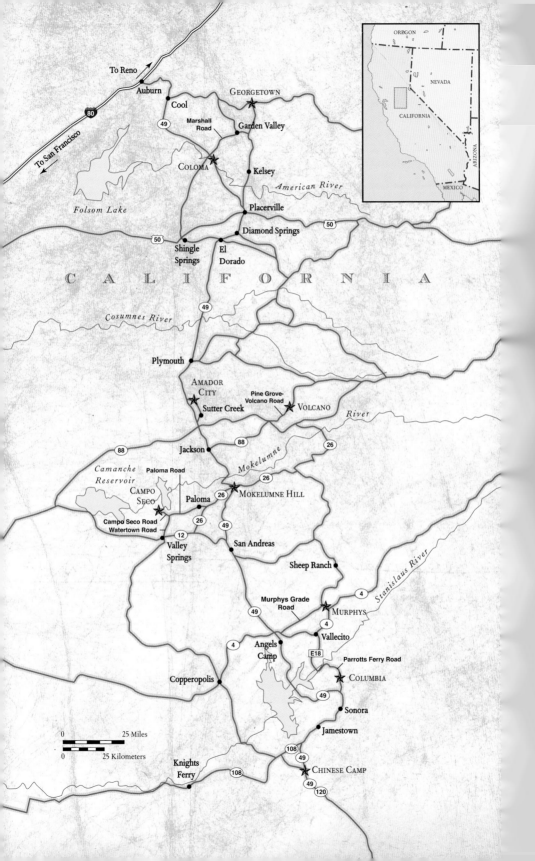

# COLOMA

Coloma is the logical place to begin California's Gold Rush history, since it was in Coloma, on January 24, 1848, that James Marshall peered into the American River. He later recalled, "My eye was caught by something shining in the bottom of the ditch. . . . It made my heart thump, for I was certain it was gold. . . . Then I saw another."

John Augustus Sutter, German-born in 1803 of Swiss parents, came to California in 1839 and became a Mexican citizen. He received a 50,000-acre land grant and was appointed the *alcalde* (a title embracing the duties of judge, lawyer, marshal, and mayor) for the entire Sacramento Valley.

His empire, which he called New Helvetia, featured a large adobe fort (still standing in Sacramento) that offered protection, food, and retail goods to nearby settlers. He also laid out a town called Sutterville, constructed a flour mill, and, providentially for California, sent James Marshall to the Coloma Valley, along the South Fork of the American River. There Marshall was to supervise the building of a sawmill, with Sutter and Marshall sharing the profits.

As sawmill construction neared completion, Marshall was inspecting the millrace, the channel through which the river would run to turn a wheel to power the sawmill. That is where he saw the glitter in the river, changing the course of California and utterly ruining Sutter's vision of a frontier agricultural dynasty.

As word of the gold discovery spread, Sutter's workers abandoned the unfinished sawmill, and his field workers and other tradesmen quit to find their fortunes. The New Helvetia that Sutter had envisioned was doomed, and Coloma became not a quiet sawmill town but a camp of frenzied Argonauts.

Because there was no law enforcement, neither Sutter nor Marshall could keep squatters out, and the banks of the American River became alive with prospectors as the gold fever spread. Although Sutter tried to profit from the fabulous find, he never did. He lamented, "What a great misfortune was this sudden gold discovery for me!" He attempted to get compensation for his lost lands, but the American courts ruled that his Mexican land grants were invalid. He eventually left New Helvetia for Pennsylvania, where he was buried in 1880.

Coloma was the first Gold Rush town, but it was hardly the richest. The river's placer deposits were depleted quickly, and the town, with a population of 5,000 in 1849, was in decline by 1851, although many of the buildings you will visit were erected after that year.

## WALKING AND DRIVING AROUND COLOMA

Most of Coloma is within Marshall Gold Discovery State Park. Begin at the visitors center—the Gold Discovery Museum—where, in addition to paying a modest fee (for admission to the museum and park, a guide booklet, and

St. John's Catholic Church, built in 1856, features an unusual bell tower that is separate from the church itself.

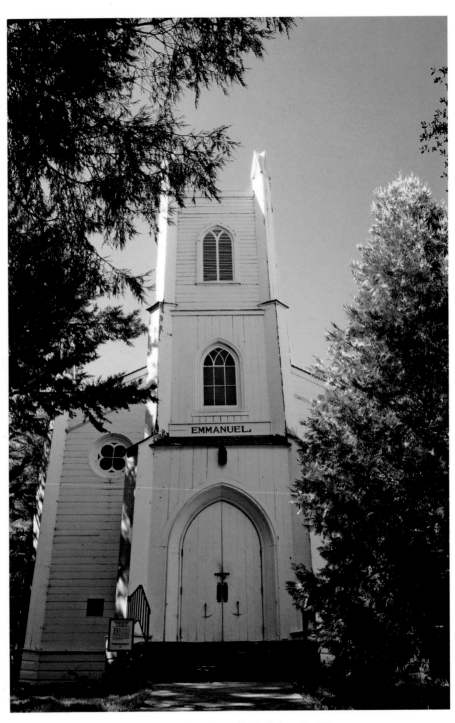

Coloma's Emmanuel Church was the site of gold discover James Marshall's funeral in 1885.

brochures), you can see exhibits of artifacts, descriptions of gold processes, and presentations of videos.

North of the gold museum are two buildings from Coloma's Chinese community. The Man Lee Store displays the techniques of placer mining, hard-rock mining, dredging, and hydraulic mining, while the Wah Hop Store retains its original purpose as a grocery and herb store (for display only).

Across the highway is a reconstruction of Sutter's Mill. The mill is not on the original site, but a nearby trail takes you there. Adjacent to the mill is the Mormon Cabin, a 1948 replica that features a short history of the Mormons who were in Coloma in 1848.

South of the sawmill on California Highway 49 are several historic buildings, some open for business. Beyond those businesses is Robert Bell's Brick Store, a general merchandise and feed store that also housed the post office. Across the

Sutter's sawmill was reconstructed in 1968 using the methods of the 1840s, with wooden pegs and hand-adzed timbers.

The Coloma Schoolhouse is a 1995 reconstruction of the building brought from Slatington in 1920, restored in 1987, but destroyed that same year by a runaway logging truck.

street but partially hidden from view is the 1854 Independent Order of Odd Fellows (I.O.O.F.) Hall.

Beyond Bell's store stands the one-room Coloma Schoolhouse. The 1890 building was brought in pieces from Slatington to Coloma in 1920. The school was completely restored in July of 1987, but, because of its location at a bend in the highway, a runaway logging truck destroyed it a mere three months later. A coalition of organizations combined their efforts to reconstruct it, completing the task in 1995.

Southwest of the visitors center are several buildings worth seeing, beginning with the 1857 stone block El Dorado County Jail, in use until 1862.

Southwest of the jail, on Church Street, stand—not surprisingly—two attractive churches. The first is the 1856 St. John's Catholic Church, where services were held until 1925. A wrought iron gate allows you an interior view. Behind the church is its cemetery. Across the road from that cemetery is a reconstruction of the cabin James Marshall built in 1856.

Down Church Street from St. John's is the 1856 Emmanuel Church, built jointly by Methodist and Episcopal congregations. James Marshall's funeral was held there in 1885. This church, like St. John's, also has an iron gate, affording you a look at its simple, unadorned interior.

At the end of Church Street is Cold Springs Road, where you will find Coloma's Pioneer Cemetery just beyond the turnoff to the James Marshall Monument. A brochure at the cemetery suggests a walking tour.

Monument Road goes to the James Marshall Monument, a bronze statue erected in 1890 that shows Marshall dramatically pointing down to the spot where he found gold. Marshall, like John Sutter, never prospered from his discovery. He spent much of his life vainly searching hills and streams for another strike. He died a bitter recluse in nearby Kelsey and is buried at the monument.

## WHEN YOU GO

*Coloma is 18 miles southeast of Auburn and 9 miles northwest of Placerville on California Highway 49.*

# GEORGETOWN

Gold was found near Georgetown, the northeastern-most town in the Mother Lode, in the summer of 1849. The camp was named for miner George Phipps. By December of that year Georgetown had a population of several thousand and a nickname—"Growlersburg," because nuggets were so large they "growled" in miners' pans.

The town received its post office in 1851. The following year, fire destroyed the thriving camp. Determined to contain future fires, town fathers moved Georgetown out of a canyon and laid out main streets a hundred feet wide, along with backstreets sixty feet wide. Citizens of the rebuilt town, which featured many brick structures with iron fire doors, triumphantly proclaimed Georgetown the "Pride of the Mountains."

Georgetown outlasted many Gold Rush camps because it had solid primary deposits, not just placer gold. In 1866 a rich vein was discovered that

The 1864 Shannon Knox residence was constructed with wood brought around Cape Horn to Georgetown, a community surrounded by a forest.

yielded $50,000 in gold in two days. Five mills with a combined thirty-five stamps were still operating in 1887, and production continued after the turn of the twentieth century.

With more than a thousand residents, Georgetown today is a livelier community than many of the area's mining camps. Several festivals and jamborees attract throngs of visitors.

## WALKING AND DRIVING AROUND GEORGETOWN

As you enter Georgetown on its hundred-foot-wide Main Street, the first building of note is on the southeast corner of Main and California Highway 193: the large, brooding, I.O.O.F. Hall, which was built in 1859 as a hotel and dance hall called the Balzar House. The architecture is rather curious, with a tall brick first story and a much shorter wooden second story. It once had a third story, which was removed in the 1890s.

Georgetown's American River Inn, formerly the American Hotel, is one of the Mother Lode's loveliest bed and breakfast inns.

Standing diagonally across from the Odd Fellows Hall is the oldest residence in town, the 1864 Shannon Knox House, which was built with wood shipped around Cape Horn—to a community surrounded by a forest.

In downtown Georgetown, on the north side of Main, stands the 1852 Wells Fargo Building; two doors east is an 1862 building that was the Civil War armory.

In the block beyond the armory are several typical Gold Rush structures—fire-resistant, single-story brick buildings with covered sidewalks and heavy iron doors.

The former American Hotel, now the American River Inn, is up the street. The most elegant building in town, the inn has been a hotel, rooming house, sanitarium, and private residence. The original 1863 hotel burned in 1897 and was rebuilt in 1899. One of the bedrooms contains a bed so tall that stepstools stand on either side to allow its occupants to get into it.

East of the main business district, in Slate Mountain Park, is a ten-stamp mill that deserves inspection, because such mills are not commonly on public display in the Mother Lode.

Georgetown's picturesque Pioneer Cemetery is located northwest of town on California Highway 193 at Greenwood Road. Headstones of immigrants from Ireland, France, Germany, Bavaria, and Switzerland demonstrate the lure of the Gold Rush. As a reminder that some mistakes are indeed "carved in stone," one elaborate marker features a misspelling—"Gone to be an Angle." In addition to the Europeans buried there are natives of Ohio, New York, Vermont, and North and South Carolina.

## WHEN YOU GO

*Georgetown is 10.6 miles northeast of Coloma. Drive 1.4 miles north from Coloma on California Highway 49 to Marshall Road for 9.1 miles and turn right (east). Follow Marshall Road through the community of Garden Valley and follow the signs to Georgetown.*

# AMADOR CITY

Amador City could pose for a photo of what visitors expect a Gold Rush mining camp to look like. It has attractive, photogenic buildings and also contains, almost hidden from view, two of the more interesting cemeteries in the Mother Lode.

Rancher José Maria Amador and several Indians camped in this area in 1848 and began placer mining. In the fall of that year, James Wheeler, a member of a gold-seeking party from Oregon, built the first cabin. Within a year, a tent camp was spread out along Amador Creek.

Imperial Hotel in Amador City was erected in 1956 and restored in 1988. Its second-story balcony has an excellent view of the business section of Amador City.

Amador City is much quieter now that new Highway 49 avoids the town. Brick and clapboard structures stand side by side on either side of the old highway.

The placer deposits had given out by 1851, but in that year four preachers found primary deposits at the Ministers' Claim, beginning the real prosperity of Amador City. Before quartz mining shut down in 1942, Amador City mines produced at least $34 million in gold.

## WALKING AND DRIVING AROUND AMADOR CITY

Because new Highway 49 now avoids Amador City, the community is a much calmer place than it was before the bypass. When you enter Amador City from the north, the business section begins at a sharp bend of the old highway. On the left stands the splendid 1879 Imperial Hotel. Originally a general merchandise store, this two-story brick building later became a hotel and served in that capacity until 1927. When I first saw the Imperial in the early 1980s, it was closed and shuttered. It was completely restored in 1988 and now elegantly serves as a hotel, restaurant, and bar.

The largest building on the east side of Old Highway 49 is the 1856 Amador Hotel. Beyond the hotel is a brick commercial building followed by a stone building housing the Amador Whitney Museum.

On the west side of the highway are five false-front commercial buildings, including the 1870s-era Chichizola General Store and the Fleehart Building.

South of the business district is the 1881 Mine House, the former Keystone Mine headquarters that is now a bed and breakfast inn. Across the street is the looming headframe of the Keystone, from which was extracted $24.5 million in gold, accounting for almost two-thirds of Amador City's total production.

To visit Amador City's two picturesque cemeteries, head east on Water Street, the road extending east from the Imperial Hotel. The first building on your left is the post office, which, at this writing, has a mannequin on the second-story balcony dressed as a Lady of the Evening, giving new meaning to the term "postmistress."

From Water Street, turn left on East School Street. Climb the hill past the library (the former schoolhouse) and turn right on Bunker Hill Road. Only 0.1 of a mile beyond the right turn, head left where Fremont Mine Road branches to the right. As you descend into a valley, you will be able to see the Oak Knoll Cemetery below. In 0.3 of a mile there is a gate on the road's west side adjacent to the house at 14501 Bunker Hill Road that leads you through a narrow field to the cemetery.

The peaceful Oak Knoll Cemetery was established in 1905, but graves predate its official standing. A wonderful verse graces the stone of Johanna Pryor, who died at age thirty-seven in 1882: "Amiable, she won all. Intelligent, she charmed all. Fervent, she loved all. And dead, she saddened all."

To visit the other cemetery, return the way you came, but before you reach the library on East School Street, turn right on Church Street, which will curve around to the south. As you pass O'Neill Street, you will see the Amador City Cemetery, in use between 1851 and 1892, on your left.

## WHEN YOU GO

*From Georgetown, take California Highway 193 for 16 miles south to Placerville. Join California Highway 49 there and go 22 miles south to Plymouth. Stay on Highway 49. South of Plymouth almost 5 miles, Old Highway 49 branches to the left from (new) Highway 49 for a 1-mile drive into Amador City.*

*Note: After you have completed your visit to Amador City, continue south on Old Highway 49 to the charming, but very commercial, town of Sutter Creek, which offers many trendy shops and upscale bed and breakfast establishments. A free, widely available walking tour will help you explore that town.*

## Jackson's Kennedy Tailings Wheels and The Kennedy Mine Tour

The town of Jackson, with a population of almost 4,000, is not included in this book, despite its attractive and historic downtown, because it has been overtaken by the twentieth and then the twenty-first centuries. It does, nevertheless, have two relics of its past that are well worth visiting.

The Argonaut and Kennedy mines were two of the most productive mines of the California Gold Rush. They were active until 1942, the year that Gold Limitation Order L-280 effectively closed mines not strategic to World War II. By the time they closed, the two mines had produced $60 million in gold.

The Argonaut is closed to the public, but one photogenic remnant of the Kennedy operation is free to the public, and the other is open on weekends for a modest price of admission.

### The Kennedy Tailings Wheels

Take Main Street north from downtown Jackson to reach the first Kennedy attraction. On your way, 0.4 of a mile north of downtown, you will pass by the 1894 St. Sava Church, the first Serbian Orthodox Church in the United States and one the loveliest houses of worship in the Gold Rush Country.

Kennedy Tailings Wheel #1 stands as a reminder of the remarkable efforts that Jackson's Kennedy Mine went through to move tailings across a valley to an impound dam. In the background at about two o'clock on the wheel is the Kennedy Mine Office.

The Kennedy Mine's headframe is the largest still standing in the Mother Lode.

Part of that beauty comes from the delicate arch over the main gate and the headstones that surround the church. Before you reach St. Sava, you will also pass three other cemeteries.

The next attraction in Jackson is 0.6 of a mile north of St. Sava. There, housed in their own park, are the enormous Kennedy Tailings Wheels. In 1912, the California state legislature passed an act requiring mines to impound their tailings, which had been polluting many of the state's streams and rivers, or cease operations within two years. This ruling had an immediate effect upon the Argonaut and Kennedy mines. The Argonaut was able to comply easily, as an impound dam could be built in a valley below the mine.

The Kennedy Mine was not as fortunate, because its only dam area was two hills away. To get the tailings to an impound dam, the Kennedy had to construct a series of lifts and flumes. The four Kennedy Tailings Wheels were the key to the operation. From an informational kiosk at the park, wheels numbers one and two are across the road to the north, and three and four are up a hill to the south.

The wheels lifted approximately 850 tons of tailings every twenty-four hours to the impound dam. The tailings moved downhill by gravity to wheel number one. The wheel, with its 208 buckets, raised the tailings forty-two feet and dropped them into a flume to wheel number two, which again raised the tailings and sent them in a long flume across the valley, the valley in which the kiosk is located, to wheel number three. The lifting process repeated twice more, after which gravity took over and sent the tailings to the dam.

The Kennedy Tailings Wheels remain an impressive sight today. Numbers one and four are still standing, while two and three are down. If you want to see how the process worked, go to wheels one and two. You can see from wheel number one's flume how it passed the tailings to number two.

If you wish to walk a shorter distance, follow the path from the kiosk to wheel number four, where you can also see the impound dam in the distance.

### The Kennedy Mine Tour

Jackson's companion attraction to the Tailings Wheels is the Kennedy Mine itself.

The Kennedy was the richest mine in this part of the Mother Lode and at one time was the deepest in the world, with a vertical shaft of 5,912 feet. It produced $35 million in gold before closing in 1942 after almost seventy-five years of operation.

The Kennedy Mine Tour is a surface tour; you do not go into the mine itself. And you would not want to, since the mine is a constant eighty-six degrees with one hundred percent humidity.

What the tour offers is an examination of more than a dozen aboveground structures, including the largest remaining headframe in the Mother Lode.

The guided tour lasts slightly more than one-and-a-half hours, enjoyable for adults but too long, I believe, for many children. You may,

A miners' room with card table stands on the third floor in the Kennedy Mine office. The table is complete with cards, chips, empty whiskey bottles, and cigars.

however, purchase a brochure that allows you to follow the tour at your own pace and, perhaps, eliminate some areas. The stamp mill, for example, is roofless and very incomplete, and you could save about twenty minutes by bypassing it.

If you have the time, however, I recommend the informative guided tour. The highlight comes at the three-story, 1907 mine office. You see the assay office and other mining-related rooms on the first floor. The second floor contains administrative offices, such as the payroll room with its imposing vault and safe—miners were paid in cash, with armed guards standing by. The third floor features living quarters.

At the end of the tour, you watch a short film made at the mine somewhere between 1914 and 1928. It is a perfect conclusion to your tour, because you will see the mine in full operation. Empty, gutted buildings like the stamp mill spring to life.

To reach the Kennedy Mine, take Highway 49 north from downtown Jackson for just over a mile, where a sign directs you to a right turn. At this writing, tours are given only on Saturday and Sunday between mid-March and October.

# VOLCANO

Volcano is one of my favorite Mother Lode mining camps. Because it is a dozen miles off Highway 49, it has relatively few visitors. It has eschewed touristy touches and remains a peaceful, lovely town with friendly citizens and many excellent buildings.

Discharged New York volunteers of the recently completed Mexican-American War discovered gold here in 1848. They called their young mining camp Volcano because they believed, erroneously, that the crater-like cup in which the town stood was volcanic. The soldiers-turned-miners even called the area's light gray-, yellow-, and reddish-colored stone "lava."

Where there was no lava, there certainly was gold. Working the placers of Soldier's Gulch, one miner netted $8,000 in a few days. Another extracted twenty-eight pounds of gold from a single pocket.

Volcano became a booming town of 5,000 citizens and could boast of such refinements as a thespian society, a debating society, a Miners' Library Association, a private law school, and an astronomical observatory, reportedly all "firsts" in California.

When placer deposits were exhausted in 1855, hydraulicking was used to uncover more gold, but the boom was over by 1865. (For more on the hydraulicking process, see either page 230 of the glossary or the North Bloomfield entry on page 72 in the next chapter.)

## WALKING AND DRIVING AROUND VOLCANO

As you enter Volcano from the southwest, you will immediately face the town's most splendid building, the St. George Hotel, a three-story brick structure with wooden porches on all floors, built sometime between 1862 and 1867.

Opposite the hotel are a small stone building and two large brick and limestone façades, the remains of the Clute Building and the Kelly and Symonds Emporium, two commercial structures that were joined together in 1861. Behind them lies Soldier's Gulch, the site of the original placer mining. Across the street stands the General Store, in continuous use since 1852, which is the hub of the goings-on in town.

East of the St. George, on the northwest corner of National and Plug streets, stands Volcano's schoolhouse, in use from 1855 until 1956, now a private residence.

North on Plug Street at Emigrant Road is St. Bernard's Catholic Church, which dates from 1854 (although it was rebuilt in 1931). On a hill northeast of the church are the town's graveyards, the Volcano Pioneer Methodist Cemetery and the Catholic cemetery.

Volcano's St. George Hotel, a three-story brick structure with wooden porches, was built somewhere between 1862 and 1867.

Volcano's Masonic Hall, built in 1860, originally housed the office of the Volcano *Weekly Ledger*.

Retrace your route on Plug Street and turn west on Consolation Street to see the wooden, two-story 1880 Union Hotel, now the Volcano Union Inn, which once went by the weighty title of the Union Hotel Billiards, Saloon, and Boarding House.

Beyond the hotel is the 1912 Armory Hall, followed by Old Abe, a bronze cannon cast in 1837 that was smuggled into Volcano in a hearse in 1862 by Union

The limestone facade of the Clute Building and the Kelly and Symonds Emporium is now the entrance to the Volcano Amphitheater.

sympathizers. As a plaque succinctly puts it, Old Abe was meant to "discourage the rebel element." During the Civil War, Volcano gold went to support the Union cause. Old Abe never fired a shot, which was just as well, since the Unionists reportedly had no cannon balls, only river rocks.

Next door to Old Abe is the Sing Kee Store, built in 1854 or 1855 as both a general merchandise and the Adams Express Agency office, the predecessor of Wells Fargo.

Attached to the back of the Sing Kee Store, but facing west, is the 1854 Masonic Hall. It originally housed the Volcano *Weekly Ledger*, with office upstairs and printing press downstairs. By 1860 the building was used by both the Masons and the Odd Fellows.

Directly across the street from the Masonic Hall is the 1871 jail. It looks rather insubstantial, with its outer walls of two-by-twelve timbers. Another identical wall is on the inside, but between the two is a layer of boilerplate. The incommodious jail features two small windows made of iron plate with small holes drilled in them.

## WHEN YOU GO

*From Jackson, head northeast on California Highway 88 to Pine Grove, a distance of 8.8 miles. Turn left on the Pine Grove-Volcano Road and follow it for 3.2 miles to Volcano.*

*Note: I saw a sign on a gas station in Pine Grove that I simply must relate to you: "Cold Beer to Go 24-Hour Pumps." I thought when I saw it that the folks in these hills are certainly serious about drinking beer.*

# MOKELUMNE HILL

In 1817, Father Narcisco Duran, writing in his diary of his exploits on the Sacramento and San Joaquin Rivers, mentioned an Indian tribe called the Muquelemnes. The name, which evolved to Mokelumne ("moe-*kull*-uh-mee"), was later given to a river you will cross coming south from Jackson on Highway 49. Miners from Oregon worked that river in 1848. A rise south of the river, where a trading post stood, was known as Mokelumne Hill.

The Gold Rush town took the name of the hill, but miners called it "Moke Hill" for short. The name was originally spelled "Mok," but "Moke" is clearly preferred in town today, probably to encourage the proper pronunciation instead of calling it "Mock" Hill.

Americans, French, Chileans, and Chinese all lived in the booming town, but the Americans, claiming property rights, eventually took over the Chilean and French claims. They apparently coexisted with the Chinese without such confrontations, as Moke Hill had a sizable Chinatown.

The community was a particularly violent place and once recorded at least one murder per week for seventeen weeks. Part of the reason for the violence might have been the simple press of humanity: the demand for mining rights was so strong that claims were restricted to a mere sixteen feet square. Miners were practically panning or digging on top of each other.

Mokelumne Hill's elegant Hotel Leger is made of brick and rhyolite tuff and dates from 1874.

A rusting but restorable Dodge truck, complete with a 1956 license plate, stands next to the stone ruins of the L. Mayer & Son Store in Mokelumne Hill.

There was plenty to pursue, however. Four Frenchmen retrieved 138 pounds of gold in a single gulch. Another miner found an 80-ounce piece of pure gold shaped like a pothook.

As the placers gave out, quartz mining and then hydraulic mining took over, but people began to exit the town in the early 1860s. Mokelumne Hill lost the Calaveras County seat in 1866.

## WALKING AND DRIVING AROUND MOKELUMNE HILL

Before you enter Mokelumne Hill on Historic Highway 49, you will pass the large Protestant Cemetery, which features a loop road. One epitaph is for William Beals, who died at age thirty-four: "His death was caused by burns received at the destruction of the Poland Hotel, San Joaquin County, on the 8th of July 1859."

Adjacent to the Protestant Cemetery is the Pioneer Jewish Cemetery, with stones dating from 1859. The markers, for natives of Germany and Prussia, are, with one exception, in both Hebrew and English.

The community of Mokelumne Hill is 0.1 of a mile beyond those cemeteries. The first buildings you will see are the roofless 1854 L. Mayer & Son Store on your left and the 1855 Wells Fargo Office, originally Levinson's Store, on your right.

Next to the Mayer building, where Center and Main Streets meet, is the 1854 I.O.O.F. Hall. Originally the two-story Adams Express Agency office, the structure, made of rhyolite tuff carved into blocks, became the first three-story building in the Mother Lode when the Odd Fellows added a story in 1861.

East of the I.O.O.F. Hall is an 1854 stone and frame commercial building known as the Italian Store. By 1889 it was owned by Chung Kee and bordered Chinatown, next door in China Gulch.

If you continue east on Center past Main through China Gulch, you will arrive at the St. Thomas Aquinas Catholic Cemetery. This graveyard also has a loop drive. Many of the stones are for natives of Ireland, France, and Italy.

Now return to Center and Main. The business district features several more historic buildings, including one of Moke Hill's loveliest structures, built in 1851 of brick and rhyolite tuff as the Hotel de France and rebuilt after an 1874 fire. It is now known as the Hotel Leger and is currently the center of activity in the community.

Down the block is the 1856 Mokelumne Hill Community Church, originally California's first Congregational Church.

To see the 1864 community school, now a private residence, turn east on Church Street from Main. Go two blocks and turn north on Old School Way. The large wooden school is easy to pick out because of its belfry.

Continue on Old School Way and turn east on Lafayette Street. On the corner of Lafayette and Marlette Streets stands the St. Thomas Aquinas Catholic Church.

## WHEN YOU GO

*From Volcano, return to Jackson. From Jackson, drive south on California Highway 49. That route bypasses Mokelumne Hill, but Historic Highway 49 (also known as Center Street) leaves the new highway 6.6 miles south of Jackson. Turn left at that point. Historic Route 49 leads to Mokelumne Hill in 0.9 of a mile.*

# CAMPO SECO

Mexicans settled Campo Seco ("dry camp") in 1849. The site was located in Oregon Gulch, named for an early group of prospectors from that territory who worked the area. But "seco" was the operant word: a thriving town in 1850, it had lost half of its population by the end of that year because scarce water sent prospectors elsewhere. In 1853, however, two Mexicans extracted $5,700 in gold in one morning in Sullivans Gulch, and, one year later, a ninety-three-ounce nugget was found, further fueling the gold frenzy. By that time the community featured two churches, the usual saloons, a brewery, two hotels, a blacksmith's shop, assorted stores, and a post office. A fire in that same year virtually destroyed the town, so many of the citizens rebuilt using stone. It is those stone buildings that offer the most interesting remnants you will see today.

Although the town was settled because of placer gold, it was the copper and zinc deposits at the Penn Mine, which opened in the 1860s and lasted until the 1940s, that provided the greatest prosperity.

## WALKING AND DRIVING AROUND CAMPO SECO

That same Penn Mine was, in the late 1990s, the site of an enormous environmental cleanup and is closed to the public. In addition, some places in the area remain off limits because it is the habitat of the endangered Valley Elderberry Longhorn Beetle. As I looked at the protective fencing and stern warnings about not disturbing the beetle, I considered how early-day miners, who ran roughshod over the land, would react to being excluded from a potential gold site by a bug.

Despite the places you can't go, there is still much to see in one of the true ghost towns of the Mother Lode. The Adams Express Agency Building, on the east side of Campo Seco Road as you enter town, provides the town's most photogenic remnants. West of those ruins on Penn Mine Road stand two mortared stone ruins that were part of the Chinese community. Surrounding these ruins are *ailanthus altissima*, the "Tree-of-Heaven" that Chinese often brought from their native land.

South of the Adams Express ruin is A. Pereira's General Store, shuttered at this writing, which served the community for decades. South of the store is another ruin with an unusual keystone-style stone lintel.

Farther south of town on the east side of the road stands an attractive Victorian home with an offset triple-bay window. Across the street, heading

The stone ruins of Campo Seco's Adams Express Agency Building are among the Mother Lode's most ghostly remnants.

west, is College Street, which leads to Campo Seco's old schoolhouse. One wonders if the town's founding fathers named the street to inspire their youth. Since my last visit, the school has been reroofed—a fine effort to protect it, except that the repairers failed to replace the school's belfry. One can only hope that the belfry is inside the school waiting to be reset.

Adjacent to the school is the Protestant cemetery, where there are more than fifty graves. One poignant epitaph is for Elizabeth Kester, who died in 1878 at thirty-eight years of age: "She sleeps in the grave with her baby."

South on Campo Seco Road 0.2 of a mile from College Street is the Catholic cemetery, where natives of Spain (including members of the Pereira family), Ireland, France, and Chile are buried.

## WHEN YOU GO

*Campo Seco is 11.7 miles southwest of Mokelumne Hill. From Main Street in Moke Hill, proceed southwest to California Highway 49. Turn left and then take an immediate right onto California Highway 26, the road to Valley Springs. In 3.8 miles, turn right on Paloma Road. In 5.5 miles, you will come to Campo Seco Road. Turn right. In 1.1 miles turn right again, which actually keeps you on Campo Seco Road, and proceed to Campo Seco, which is a mile away.*

# MURPHYS

Murphys is another of my favorite Gold Rush mining camps. With streets lined with locust trees, its central business district invites a stroll. In fact, staying the night and walking Murphys' streets in the evening is a requirement for each of my Mother Lode visits.

Murphys is named for John M. Murphy, who came to California from Canada in 1844. Four years later, John and his brother Daniel camped along Angels Creek at a place later known as Murphys New Diggings—but shortened to Murphys when it received a post office in 1851. By that time, the Murphy brothers were long gone. They opened a trading post to sell to the hordes of hopeful miners, made their fortune, and left town in 1849.

Early claims were restricted to a tiny eight-foot square; nevertheless, one claim is said to have yielded thirty-seven pounds of gold in a single afternoon and another sixty-three pounds the following morning.

Murphys' peak year was 1855, but, like dozens of other camps, the town began declining in the 1860s despite attempts at hard-rock and hydraulic mining.

## WALKING AND DRIVING AROUND MURPHYS

Main Street features a number of excellent buildings, with the most obvious the rough-quarried limestone Murphys Hotel, at the southwest corner of Main and Algiers Streets. It opened in 1856 as the Sperry and Perry Hotel and was later known as Mitchler's Hotel. It became the Murphys Hotel in 1945. The hotel has a register containing the names of some of America's most famous figures: Mark Twain, Horatio Alger Jr., J. Pierpont Morgan, and Ulysses S. Grant. It also features one of California's most infamous: Charles E. Bolton, the highwayman Black Bart.

Diagonally across from the hotel is the former Jones' Apothecary Shop. Constructed after an 1859 fire, it was built never to burn: in addition to its limestone and brick walls and iron doors, it has windows only on its one street-facing wall. It later became the I.O.O.F. Hall and in 1886 became Ben and James Stephens' store. An old painted sign on the building's west side announces that business: "Stephens Bro's. Cheap Cash Store."

West on Main and across from a modern section of the Murphys Hotel is the 1856 Peter L. Traver Building, which features a Gold Rush–era museum open Friday through Sunday. Attached to the Traver Building on the west is the Thompson Building, built around 1856. On its western exterior wall is the amusing and anecdotal Wall of

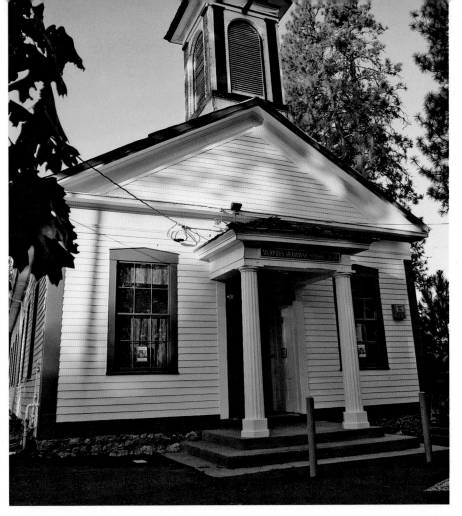

The former Murphys Grammar School, built in 1860, was in use until 1973. It was called the "Pine Grove College" by its students.

Comparative Ovations, which commemorates pioneers and honorable members of E Clampus Vitus, a mock-serious benevolent brotherhood that erects historical plaques throughout the West. The organization, a burlesque (beginning with its pseudo-Latin name) of secret fraternal orders, began in California during the Gold Rush and was revived in the 1930s. Its members have debated whether it is an "Historical Drinking Society" or a "Drinking Historical Society." I confess to being a member of the brotherhood, but I decline to take a position in this debate.

St. Patrick's Catholic Church is located 0.2 of a mile north of the business district at 619 Sheep Ranch Road. A plaque states that the church was originally located near Jones' Apothecary Shop. That building was destroyed by fire, but "...the chalice and other sacred appurtenances were carried to safety by 'Auntie'

The 1856 Murphys Hotel features a still-popular saloon, a dining room featuring excellent meals, and an upstairs of completely restored rooms. Think twice before choosing a room above the saloon on weekends.

The Presidential Suite in the Murphys Hotel honors its most famous occupant, President Ulysses S. Grant.

St. Patrick's Catholic Church in Murphys, dedicated in 1861, features precise brick work and lancet windows.

Moran in her voluminous apron." The attractive church was begun in 1858 and dedicated in 1861. A well-kept cemetery is within the church grounds.

To visit another cemetery, head east from downtown Murphys on Main. Jones Street veers off to the right behind a large monument. Follow Jones for 0.2 of a mile to the turnoff to the Buena Vista Cemetery, which has hundreds of graves in a pleasant, tree-lined setting.

Immediately east of the cemetery entrance is the former Murphys Grammar School. Built in 1860, it was continuously in use until 1973. It was called "Pine Grove College" by its pupils, one of whom, physicist Albert Michelson, was the first American to win a Nobel Prize.

## WHEN YOU GO

*From Campo Seco, return the way you came, but only for 1 mile. Then turn south on Watertown Road, which will lead you in 2.7 miles to the community of Valley Springs and California Highway 12. From there, take that road east to California Highway 49, a distance of 8.2 miles. Then drive south on Highway 49 for 12.2 miles to a left turn onto Murphys Grade Road. That turnoff is 1 mile north of Angels Camp, so if you enter Angels Camp, you have missed the turn. Murphys is 6.5 miles northeast from the left turn onto Murphys Grade Road off of Highway 49.*

# COLUMBIA

During the Gold Rush, the town of Columbia was hailed as the "Gem of the Southern Mines." More than 150 years later, the "gem" remains unflawed. Now a state park, Columbia features attractions like restaurants, shops, stagecoach rides, a hotel, a theater, and even a saloon. But despite all this activity, Columbia retains a dignity that makes it a most enjoyable place.

The Mother Lode consisted of one incredible place to find gold after another, but fortuitous Columbia is geologically unique: it sits on a limestone bed pockmarked with potholes that for thousands of years conveniently collected placer gold, seemingly waiting for someone to retrieve it.

That someone was Dr. Thaddeus Hildreth, who in 1850 camped in the area with a group of prospectors. The gold was so plentiful that others swarmed to the new camp, first called Hildreth's Diggings, later American Camp, and finally Columbia.

Despite an acute shortage of water (eventually solved with an elaborate series of flumes and ditches), Columbia prospered wildly, becoming a town of 6,000—the biggest camp in the Mother Lode. Although Columbia now has the permanence of brick, it began, like other mining camps, as a mere tent city with an occasional rough-sawn wood structure. After fires in 1854 and 1857, it was rebuilt with locally made brick and fireproof iron doors shipped from eastern states.

As placer gold gave out in the 1860s, Columbia declined. By the 1880s its population had dropped to about five hundred, but not before an estimated $87 million in gold had been shipped from the Gem of the Southern Mines.

## WALKING AROUND COLUMBIA

Columbia retains its Gold Rush atmosphere better than any other sizable Mother Lode town. One reason is that automobiles are not allowed within its interior streets. Another is that shops selling wares are not permitted to display gaudy, touristy signs.

A third reason Columbia is so delightful is that it is a living history museum (with no admission fee) where shopkeepers dress in period attire, a strolling folk singer plays traditional instruments while singing nineteenth-century songs, and a blacksmith uses hundred-year-old tools to create his wares. You can ride in an authentic stagecoach, watch a play, or stay the night in the 1856 City Hotel (closed at this writing but "opening soon," according to a Columbia website).

Columbia's Wells Fargo office, built in 1858 by William Daegner, was in service until 1917.

Columbia has too many attractions to list them all, but I found the most enjoyment in buildings in which there was little or nothing for sale, such as the 1858 Wells Fargo Express Building on the south end of Main Street, which has a chalkboard announcing the stages "arriving" and "departing" as well as freight ready to be "shipped."

You need to explore Columbia carefully to see more than the obvious attractions. For example, hidden behind the Wells Fargo Building is a well-equipped assay office that would be easy to overlook.

The two largest "ghost town" state parks in California are Columbia and Bodie (see page 146). The principal difference between them is exemplified in Columbia's Franco cabin at the southwest corner of Main and Jackson Streets. When you look through this cabin's windows, you see a home ready for a drill sergeant's inspection:

The Columbia Schoolhouse has an outside staircase, barely in view on the far right, to reach the second-story classroom

The first-floor classroom of the Columbia Schoolhouse shows a map of the Americas—and a dunce cap awaiting an unprepared student.

clothes are hung on hooks; dishes are neatly stacked; the bed is made. On a small table is an unfinished "letter": "My Dear Wife, I take pen in hand to tell you about my fortunes in the. . . ." One almost expects Mr. Franco to appear through a doorway.

Bodie is vastly different. The same cabin there would have items left scattered about in abandonment: a bed with no mattress, a child's broken toy, and dust everywhere. No one can mistake a Bodie cabin for one that has life.

Personally, I am very glad the two state parks are so different, as each has a distinct feel for history. It is wonderful not to have to choose between the two.

An often-overlooked building is the 1860 two-classroom Columbia Schoolhouse. An enjoyable way to reach it is on foot, taking the "Old School Trail" from Pacific

Columbia's St. Charles Saloon still offers alcoholic beverages, but its clientele is now considerably more family oriented than it was during the Gold Rush.

and Columbia Streets. The attractive two-story brick building last saw students in 1937, when it was deemed unsafe should an earthquake occur.

Behind the schoolhouse are three of Columbia's four cemeteries: the public cemetery (with "In God We Trust" on a wooden arch over the entrance) and adjacent graveyards for the Masons and Odd Fellows. (The fourth, a Catholic cemetery, stands south of town next to St. Anne's Church on Kennebec Hill.)

In the public cemetery stands an interesting matching pair of headstones. The first is for Joel A. Cumback, who died in 1857 at age thirty. The stone was erected by his friend, Jacob R. Giddis. Next to Cumback's grave lies that friend, who was murdered four years later at age twenty-eight.

## WHEN YOU GO

*From downtown Murphys, head east on Main Street for 0.4 of a mile to its junction with California Highway 4. Follow that highway for 3.3 miles and turn left on Parrotts Ferry Road. That road will take you to Columbia in 9.8 miles.*

# CHINESE CAMP

Chinese Camp is the other true ghost town in the Mother Lode, along with Campo Seco (see page 46). For that reason alone, it is well worth a visit. In addition, its Main Street absolutely invites a sketchpad.

Chinese Camp was the oldest town populated by Chinese, settled in 1849 at a place first known as Washington Camp. Later called Chinese Diggings and then Chinese (or even Chinee) Camp, it received its post office in 1854. By that time, it had a population of 5,000, as many as half of them non-Asian.

Although the Chinese were targets of discrimination, that did not mean they were always a united people. Secret societies called "tongs," based upon one's home area in China, were prevalent where there were large numbers of Chinese.

Two of those tongs had a violent skirmish near Chinese Camp in 1856, apparently caused by a large rock rolling from one group's diggings into the other's. The subsequent Tong War, as it came to be known, involved over 2,000 men wielding daggers, axes, spears, and even a few muskets. Four men died during the resulting mayhem, and 250 were jailed afterward.

Placer mining at Chinese Camp lasted into the 1870s and yielded an estimated $2.5 million in gold. The town also served as an important transportation hub.

## WALKING AROUND CHINESE CAMP

Chinese Camp today consists of almost a dozen buildings in various states of decay among a proliferation of ailanthus trees—the traditional Chinese "Tree-of-Heaven," a highly invasive species that is difficult to control or eradicate.

The Chinese Camp Store stands prominently near the intersection of California Highway 49 and California Highway 120. Go south from the store to a historical monument and park there, as the town's Main Street is around the corner.

The first commercial building on the north side of the street is the 1854 Timothy McAdams Store, which served as both a general store and the post office. Its postal boxes were accessible from the outside.

Next door to the McAdams Store is a two-story wooden residence that was a doctor's home, office, and boarding house. Across the street is one standing wall of the 1849 office of the Adams Express Agency, later Wells Fargo. Its iron doors now reside in the Wells Fargo Museum in San Francisco. West of that wall was a building, now gone, that was a combination livery stable and brewery. (One

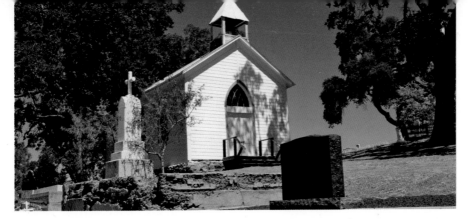

Chinese Camp's St. Francis Xavier Catholic Church, built in 1855, features a cemetery with about a dozen old graves, most for natives of Ireland.

wonders if they had the area's happiest horses or its worst-tasting beer.)

Next door to the doctor's house is a brick building with iron doors that was a foundry and blacksmith shop. John Studebaker, who later made wheelbarrows for miners in Coloma and Placerville before becoming an Indiana automobile builder, learned his trade in that shop, according to a town resident.

Across the street from the foundry is the Buck Store, a stone building with a wooden false front. Next door is a large, two-story, wood-frame structure on the corner of Main Street and Red Hills Road that was a fandango parlor and house of prostitution.

East of Highway 49 on Main Street is the attractive 1855 St. Francis Xavier Catholic Church and Cemetery, with about a dozen old graves, most for natives of Ireland.

Although Chinese were the town's principal residents, one would not expect to find graves of Chinese there: it was tradition to return their remains to their native land. California law, however, required their burial for sanitary reasons. The remains had to stay buried for three years, but for a four-year period after that, the remains could be disinterred and shipped to China. During that four-year time frame, Chinese societies and organizations, including the tongs, made certain that remains were properly disinterred and returned to China.

## WHEN YOU GO

*From Columbia, follow Parrotts Ferry Road south for 1.9 miles until it meets California Highway 49. Continue 2.3 miles into Sonora. Chinese Camp is 10.2 miles southwest of Sonora on Highway 49.*

# 2

# GHOSTS

O F   T H E

# NORTHERN
MINES

DESPITE THE FAME OF THE MOTHER LODE, the greatest concentration of lode gold came from an area north of Auburn, a place referred to by the miners themselves as the "Northern Mines." The richest of those mines, located in Nevada County, were not the small-time workings of hardy prospectors but rather the province of investors with deep pockets and owners with enormous capital at stake. These mines were among the longest-lasting and best-producing in California. Nevada County, with $440 million, produced more than twice as much gold between 1848 and 1965 as any other California county.

Your tour of the Northern Mines begins in Grass Valley, twenty-five miles north of Auburn, which has an historic downtown business district filled with Gold Rush–era buildings. Unfortunately, it is also filled with people and automobiles. Like several larger towns in Chapter 1, Grass Valley simply is too much of this century and not enough of the nineteenth for inclusion in this book. Nevertheless, I recommend walking its downtown area (a free tour booklet is widely available). The town's star attraction is the Empire Mine State Park (see page 66).

A reconstruction of the Johnsville Firehouse, completed in 1967, recalls the building's 1908 appearance.

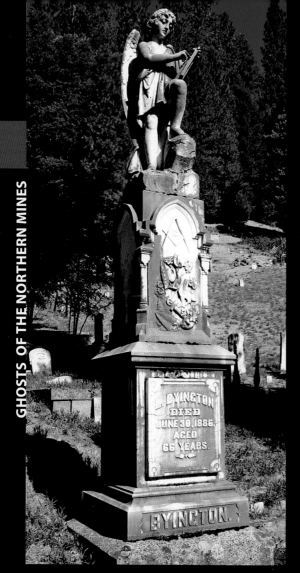

In Downieville, an angel with his harp decorates the elaborate headstone for L. Byington, who died in 1886.

But the farther one gets from Grass Valley, the more charming and ghostly the entries in this chapter become. Nevada City, Grass Valley's sister community, has an excellent concentration of fine buildings. Dutch Flat is only a couple of miles off Interstate 80, but it has a true back roads ambience. North Bloomfield is a state park and has been preserved as a genuine, historic ghost town surrounded by an environmental catastrophe. Even farther along the back roads of Northern California are three enchanting communities with photogenic buildings and scenery: Downieville, Sierra City, and Johnsville. When you have visited all these towns of the Northern Mines, you will feel a century removed from the freeways of California's largest cities.

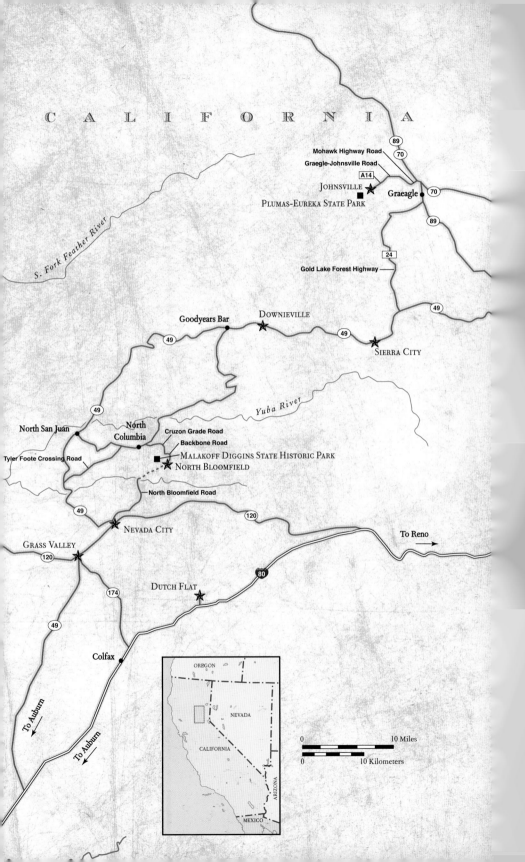

CALIFORNIA

89
70

Mohawk Highway Road
Graegle-Johnsville Road
A14
JOHNSVILLE ★  Graeagle ● 70
PLUMAS-EUREKA STATE PARK

89

24

Gold Lake Forest Highway

49

Goodyears Bar ●  DOWNIEVILLE ★    49
49  SIERRA CITY ★

Yuba River

49

North San Juan    North
Columbia    Cruzon Grade Road
Backbone Road
Tyler Foote Crossing Road    ■ MALAKOFF DIGGINS STATE HISTORIC PARK
★ NORTH BLOOMFIELD

North Bloomfield Road

49    120

NEVADA CITY ★    To Reno →

GRASS VALLEY ★
120    80

DUTCH FLAT ★
174

49

Colfax ●

S. Fork Feather River

To Auburn
To Auburn

OREGON
NEVADA
CALIFORNIA
ARIZONA
MEXICO

0                    10 Miles
0                    10 Kilometers

# NEVADA CITY

When an unknown prospector found placer gold where Nevada City would later stand, he named his spot Deer Creek Dry Diggings. Later it would be called Caldwell's Upper Store for Dr. A. B. Caldwell's trading post. Finally it became Nevada and then, when it was incorporated in 1851, City of Nevada. By 1858 it was widely known as Nevada City.

Nevada City likely provided the name for California's eastern neighbor, as Nevada territory was named in 1861, long after Nevada City was already a thriving community. Furthermore, the Washoe silver rush was started by Nevada City miners who had ventured east over the Sierra Nevada and brought back ore samples. When "Nevada" was finalized for the new state, Nevada City residents protested, saying they had the name first.

According to the 1850 census, Nevada City had a population of 1,067. But by the end of that year, it had risen to 6,000 citizens as miners flocked to an area where gold veins did not pinch out as usual but rather widened into remarkable primary deposits. Miners would burrow into the hills, in a process that became known as "coyoteing" after the digging prowess of that canine.

Nevada City's Nevada Theatre featured performances by such notables as Mark Twain and Jack London.

Nevada City women staged a grand ball to raise money for the construction of Pennsylvania Engine Co. No. 2, which was finished in 1861.

The National Hotel in Nevada City claims to be the oldest continuously operated hotel in California. Note the lovely wrought iron railings on the third-floor balconies.

The New York Hotel in Nevada City displays its delicate latticework and elegant wood trim.

Nevada City's 1864 Methodist Church has an offset bell tower. Note how the window above the entrance is echoed in design by the window in the bell tower itself.

The town's population rose to 10,000 by the late 1850s, when Nevada City was "Queen of the Northern Mines" and the third-largest California city. But Nevada City was already in decline by the end of the decade, with many prospectors heading east to the silver excitement of the Nevada Territory's Comstock Lode.

# WALKING AND DRIVING AROUND NEVADA CITY

Nevada City's entire downtown business section is a National Historic District. The primary street to explore is Broad Street, but a good place to start a walking tour is at the Chamber of Commerce, located one block north of Broad Street where Commercial, Main, Union, and Coyote Streets all converge. There you can obtain a free walking tour guide.

A logical second stop is a few doors northwest on Main at the 1861 Nevada Hose Company No. 1, a graceful two-story structure with delicate carpenter's lace gingerbread trim. It currently houses a museum that contains many Native American baskets and tools, a large display of Chinese artifacts, and an eclectic assortment of household items.

On Broad Street you will find the largest concentration of interesting buildings, beginning with the 1856–57 National Hotel, an elegant amalgamation of three three-story brick buildings on the east end of the business district. Up the street stands the 1859 Nevada Theatre, where such notables as Mark Twain and Jack London appeared. Across the street are the 1861 Firehouse No. 1 and the 1880s New York Hotel, now a series of shops.

The lovely 1864 Methodist Church stands where Broad Street begins a turn to the northwest and becomes West Broad Street (with East Broad Street branching from it about three hundred feet north of the church). Beyond that church 0.3 of a mile on West Broad Street is St. Canice Catholic Cemetery, which features excellent marble headstones, many for natives of Ireland and Italy.

Immediately south of that graveyard is the 1851 Pioneer Cemetery. The tallest marker gave me chills of admiration. It is for Henry Meredith, born in Virginia in 1826. He died in a battle with Paiute Indian warriors at Pyramid Lake, Utah Territory (now Nevada), in 1860. His epitaph reads, "Brave, gifted, generous, and faithful, he closed a life of usefulness and purity by a death of honor." What created the chills were his last words, also on the marker: "No. Leave me here. I'm going to put you in peril." Wounded, he said this to others who offered to help him from the field.

## WHEN YOU GO

*Nevada City is 4 miles north of Grass Valley on California Highway 49 and California Highway 120. Take the Broad Street Exit.*

## Grass Valley's Empire Mine State Historic Park and North Star Mining Museum

The Empire Mine is a fine place to learn about the fundamentals of the mining process. You can peer down the Empire shaft, which drops almost a mile into the earth. You can observe the machine shop, which has an array of tools and the smell of oil and metal. You can walk through the mine company offices, where officials oversaw the operation of Grass Valley's richest mine, which was in production from 1850 until 1956 and brought forth, at today's prices, more than $2 billion in gold.

You can also view the rewards of that successful mining operation by touring the Bourn "Cottage," a summer country home most people would consider a mansion. One treat at the Bourn Cottage occurs on weekends from spring until fall, when historic recreations of scenes from the mine owners' lives are presented.

To visit the Empire Mine, leave California Highway 49 at the Marysville/Empire Street exit. Follow Empire Street east to the park entrance, a distance of 1.3 miles.

The office of Mine Superintendent George Starr contains ore specimens and a secure-looking safe made in Los Angeles.

The 1897 Bourn "Cottage" was so called because the Bourn family, who owned the Empire Mine, had several other larger homes. Notice, when you visit the empire mine, that the mine company office uses the same stone and brick materials as the Cottage, albeit on a less grand scale.

A second excellent Grass Valley attraction is the North Star Mining Museum, which contains some of California's best mining memorabilia. A collection of gold ore from throughout the Mother Lode is one highlight. One of the museum's more unusual acquisitions is an 1899 dynamite packing machine.

But its most dramatic attraction is a huge Pelton wheel, the largest in the world when it was installed at this former powerhouse in 1896. A Pelton wheel utilizes the force of a turbine-directed jet of water to turn buckets on the periphery of the wheel to produce electric power. It was named for its inventor, Lester A. Pelton, who patented the device in 1880.

To visit the North Star Mining Museum from the Empire Mine, return west on Empire Street to California Highway 49, cross the freeway, and take an immediate right turn, which will double back under the highway as Allison Ranch Road. The museum will be in front of you across Courtney Street.

# DUTCH FLAT

Dutch Flat seems like an ideal place to live. Although it is easily accessible to large communities via the nearby interstate, it truly resides in its past. At an elevation of 3,144 feet, it is cooler than many of the sites in Gold Country but still low enough to avoid a serious winter. Furthermore, unlike many Gold Rush camps, Dutch Flat never had a major fire, so it remains a lovely and well-preserved nineteenth-century town.

German prospectors and merchants Charles and Joseph Dornbach began placer mining here in 1851 and called the place Dutch Charlie's Flat. The name was shortened to Dutch Flat when the town received its post office in 1856. When hydraulic mining began in 1857, the community's population grew to about 2,000 citizens; in 1860 the town had the largest number of voters in Placer County. When the Central Pacific Railroad was being constructed, as many as 2,000 Chinese also lived in Dutch Flat, but they naturally moved on as the railroad progressed. The town was well known during the 1860s because the Central Pacific called their chosen path for the transcontinental railroad the "Dutch Flat Route."

By 1867, forty-five hydraulic mines were operating within a mile and a half of town. It also was the first location in which newly invented dynamite was extensively utilized in mining.

Like many other Northern Mine towns, Dutch Flat's prosperous times ended when hydraulicking was virtually halted in 1884, but not before producing an estimated $5 million in gold. (For more on the hydraulic process, see the next entry in this chapter.)

## WALKING AND DRIVING AROUND DUTCH FLAT

As you approach Dutch Flat, you will enter a lovely valley with several pleasant homes (and no "flat" to be seen). When you turn onto Main Street, you enter into a beautiful, quiet town that features several excellent historic buildings shaded by poplar and locust trees. On your left is the 1858 two-story I.O.O.F. Hall made of stone block, with tin covering its side walls. The lower floor contained H. R. Hudepohl's store.

Next door is the 1856 Masonic Lodge, which has a stone first floor and clapboard second story. Across the street from the lodge is the three-story Dutch Flat Hotel. Originally a one-story hotel, it was built in 1852.

A half-mile walk (or drive) takes you to Dutch Flat's two attractive cemeteries. Go north on Main to Fifth Avenue, turn right, and then turn left onto Cemetery

Methodist Episcopal Church in Dutch Flat was completed in 1861 and is still in use.

Road. The first graveyard is the public one, which sits underneath a canopy of trees and within a carpet of lush ferns.

You can walk through the northeast exit of the public cemetery to the Masonic and I.O.O.F. cemeteries, which are side-by-side up the road. The largest marker is for German-born Herman R. Hudepohl (1828–1896), the man who had the store beneath the I.O.O.F. Hall. Incidentally, he played no favorites—he was a Mason as well as an Odd Fellow.

When I took this photo of the Dutch Flat School, now a community center, the town was preparing for its annual White Elephant Sale, which raises money for the maintenance of the former school.

As you return on Cemetery Street to Fifth Avenue, you can see the rear of one of Dutch Flat's most elegant buildings, the Methodist Episcopal Church. To visit it, turn left on Fifth and left again on Stockton. The wood-frame church, which was begun in 1859 and completed in 1861 and is still in use, has more ornate carving on its face and steeple than most churches in Gold Rush Country.

Dutch Flat's I.O.O.F. Hall, left, is made of stone and block, with tin covering its side walls; the Masonic Lodge to its right features a stone first floor and a clapboard second story.

Directly across from the church is another gem, the Dutch Flat School, now a community center. The first floor features two classrooms, while the second story has an auditorium.

You passed another historic building as you were entering town, but it was very easy to miss, so you can examine it as you leave Dutch Flat. Continue on Stockton past the school as the street turns south and intersects with Sacramento, your street into town. This time turn left. Almost immediately on your left will be an 1870 Chinese store, which is made of solid adobe, not adobe bricks.

When you leave Dutch Flat and return to Ridge Road, this time go onto I-80 heading west and get off almost immediately at the rest area, which is actually built on the site of one of the mining district's major hydraulic operations, the Stewart Mine. At the rest area are several informative plaques and a hydraulic monitor.

## WHEN YOU GO

*From Grass Valley, take California Highway 174 southeast for 14 miles to Colfax (which features several historic buildings in its business district). Take Interstate 80 east (actually northeast) for 10 miles and exit on Ridge Road. Turn left (west) and follow the signs to Dutch Flat, less than 2 miles away.*

# NORTH BLOOMFIELD AND MALAKOFF DIGGINS STATE HISTORIC PARK

North Bloomfield is the premier ghost town of the Northern Mines. Now a state historic park, it moves at a much slower pace than the other three more famous state park mining towns: Coloma, Columbia, and Bodie. Some Gold Country tour books consider North Bloomfield a "side trip." Not so—it is the *destination*.

Early prospectors in the North Bloomfield area were disappointed in their findings along a stream and so named it Humbug Creek. When a camp formed nevertheless, the community was called Humbug. Despite the moniker, the town prospered. When a post office was granted, the town was hardly a "humbug," and citizens chose Bloomfield as its name. The Postal Service required the addition of "North," because another Bloomfield already existed in California (and it still does, southwest of Santa Rosa).

The reason the camp went from a "humbug" to a town of 2,000 citizens was the invention of hydraulic mining. In 1853 local prospector Edward Matteson used a rawhide hose and a wooden nozzle to wash gold-laden ore from a bluff. Matteson's invention drastically changed the gold mining industry. His wooden nozzle was

A hydraulic monitor, also known as a "giant," sits in the bottom of the Malakoff Mine.

refined into a metal cannon-like contraption called a "monitor" or "giant" that propelled water with incredible force into gravel banks containing gold. The gold was exposed and separated, while the water, which eventually was brought to North Bloomfield through forty-three miles of flumes and ditches, washed away the waste.

As a result, gold that had been impenetrably locked in gravel became highly profitable to mine. An estimated $4.5 million in gold was retrieved from only two of the area's many mines. At one of them, the Malakoff, gold was smelted on site. The largest bar weighed 510 pounds and was valued at $114,000, the richest bar ever shipped from Nevada County.

The process was almost too easy—if it had not been for hydraulicking's aftereffects. The mines themselves were denuded of vegetation, and enormous amounts of waterborne detritus created environmental havoc downstream. Silt in rivers caused floods, killed fish and riparian wildlife, destroyed farmlands, and hampered navigation as far away as San Francisco Bay.

For ten years, concerned Californians waged a legal battle against powerful financial interests to halt the devastation. In 1884 a federal court finally ordered a halt to the wholesale dumping of tailings, effectively eliminating most hydraulic mining—and effectively emptying North Bloomfield.

This view of the Malakoff Diggins clearly shows where the hydraulic monitors washed the hillsides, releasing a fortune in gold—but causing environmental havoc downstream.

This ghostly interior photo of St. Columncille's Catholic Church in North Bloomfield was taken through one of its windows.

North Bloomfield's McKillican and Mobley General Merchandise was the social center for the town. It also housed the post office, which closed in 1941.

The McKillican and Mobley General Merchandise featured everything from household items to livery equipment.

The King's Saloon was erected in the early 1870s. The Smith and Knotwell Drugstore, with a Masonic Lodge on the second floor, is a reconstruction of the original.

## WALKING AND DRIVING AROUND NORTH BLOOMFIELD

North Bloomfield today is a picturesque town of picket fences, shade trees, small but pleasant single-story clapboard homes, and several attractive wood-frame commercial buildings.

Park headquarters is Cummins Hall—a former dance hall and saloon, containing a well-stocked museum and an informative video on hydraulic mining. Here you pay a modest admission price to the park.

Next door is the reconstructed Kallenberger Barber Shop and, beyond, the tiny King's Saloon, built in the early 1870s. Next door to the saloon is a reconstruction of the two-story Masonic Lodge with the Smith and Knotwell Drugstore on its first floor.

Across the street stands the 1870 McKillican and Mobley General Merchandise. This building contains new-old-stock items and the town's post office, featuring a convenient outdoor mail drop.

West of town 0.4 of a mile is the 1860 St. Columncille's Catholic Church. It originally was located northeast of French Corral, now a minor ghost town about thirteen air miles southwest of North Bloomfield. In its original location, it first served as the Bridgeport Union Guard Hall before becoming a church in 1869. It was moved to this location, the site of an earlier Catholic church, in 1971.

King's Saloon in North Bloomfield extols its honesty with a sign at the rear of the establishment: "This is a square house. Please report any unfairness to the proprietor."

Next door to St. Columncille's is the 1872–1873 North Bloomfield School, a large, two-room L-shaped building that allowed for a teachers' nightmare: about forty desks are set up in one of the rooms. The school last had students in 1941.

Behind the church is a small, well-kept cemetery with graves of people from, among other places, Illinois, Virginia, Minnesota, Vermont, Ireland, Switzerland, and Germany. Across the street from the church is a path that takes you a short distance through a manzanita grove to an overlook of the Le Du hydraulic mine.

But that view pales in comparison to the sight that awaits you 0.4 of mile west of the church and school at the Malakoff Diggins. Park your car and take the 240-foot trail to the overlook.

A five-minute walk beyond that overlook gives you an even better view of the "diggins." The colors of the denuded hills range from slate gray to tan to tawny brown. If it were natural, we'd think it was beautiful, because it has an otherworldly appearance, rather like Utah's Bryce Canyon. We are reminded that this is unnatural, however, by a stream running through the diggins with water disturbingly darker than it should be.

Beyond the main diggins site 0.2 of a mile on North Bloomfield Road is the West Point Overlook, where a short hike takes you down to a water pipe and its monitor. This short but somewhat steep trail goes into the mine itself, giving you a genuine feel for how the hydraulicking process can alter the environment.

## WHEN YOU GO

From Dutch Flat, return to Grass Valley and then go 4 miles north on California Highway 49 and California Highway 120 and take the Broad Street Exit into Nevada City. The more "tame" route to North Bloomfield is this one: From Nevada City, head to California Highway 49, which you can do by simply driving north from the Nevada City cemeteries on West Broad Street for about 0.2 of a mile. Turn left on Highway 49 and drive for 10 miles to Tyler Foote Crossing Road. Turn right and proceed for 8.1 miles to North Columbia, which features a delightful former schoolhouse. A mile and a half beyond North Columbia, turn right onto Cruzon Grade (it becomes the main road and Tyler Foote Crossing the lesser). Cruzon Grade will dovetail into Backbone Road. In 5.7 miles from North Columbia, turn right on Derbec Road, which in 0.7 of a mile will meet North Bloomfield Road. Turn right and proceed 1.3 miles to North Bloomfield. That's a total distance of almost 28 miles from Nevada City.

There is, however, another option from Nevada City, a much more direct, and lovelier, route, although it is probably slower (despite the lower mileage) than the way described above. From Broad Street (the principal thoroughfare of Nevada City), head northwest past the Methodist Church. About three hundred feet from the church, Broad Street branches into West Broad and East Broad Streets. At that point, take the right fork and proceed about 0.3 of a mile until you reach California Highway 49. Directly across Highway 49 is North Bloomfield Road, and it is so marked. Follow that road for 14.3 miles to the townsite. The route is a twisting, winding, and narrow road, although a passenger car can certainly make the drive. If you love the back roads, you will relish this route, which includes a dramatic view of the South Yuba River from a one-lane bridge. (The road goes from paved to dirt at that point, with 5.4 miles left to go to North Bloomfield.) You will enter Malakoff Diggins State Park and the vista points described above before you reach the ghost town of North Bloomfield.

**Important Note:** This state park is the first in this book that was slated to close in 2012 due to budgetary shortfalls. What that probably means is that the museum will be closed. I can't imagine how they could deny you access to the Malakoff Diggins or the road through North Bloomfield itself, since that is a dedicated public road. But it would be a good idea to go to the website given on page 13 to determine the status of this state park before you plan a visit.

# DOWNIEVILLE

Downieville is my favorite town in all of Northern California. During the week it is a somnolent, delightful community replete with friendly people, well-kept historic buildings, good restaurants, and enjoyable accommodations. On weekends, something always seems to be happening—mountain bike festivals, fly-fishing activities, kayaking expeditions, motorcycle rallies, E Clampus Vitus "doins"—you name it. But whether the place is sleeping or jumping, there is one constant: the entrancing sound of rushing water from either the Downie or the Yuba River, which have a confluence right in town. I stay in a room directly above the Downie, and there is nothing like falling asleep with the tranquilizing rumbles of the river.

That confluence of the Yuba and a then-unnamed river yielded placer gold in the fall of 1849. The settlement that grew at the discovery site was variously called Jim Crow Diggins, Washingtonville, Missouri Town, and The Forks. The community settled on the name Downieville for Scotsman William Downie, its leading citizen. On Christmas Day of that year, Downie, who had proclaimed himself a major, climbed onto a cabin roof armed with a flag and a pistol. The major later wrote, "I made a short speech, waved the flag, and fired a few shots and finished up by giving three cheers for the American Constitution." Merry Christmas!

Just beyond the St. Charles Place Saloon in Downieville, Highway 49 turns to one lane as it crosses the Downie River.

By May of the next year, Downieville had fifteen hotels and gambling houses along with four butcher shops and four bakeries. By the next year, it had 5,000 citizens.

Placer mining yielded to quartz and even hydraulic mining, but the excitement was over by 1867. One exception was the Gold Bluff Mine, which was worked sporadically into the 1950s, producing about $1.5 million in gold.

## WALKING AND DRIVING AROUND DOWNIEVILLE

You will likely be coming into Downieville from the west, and that's too bad, because the far more pleasant entrance is from the east. When you enter town coming from Sierra City, you slowly pass attractive residences, an 1850s protestant church, and an 1864 Masonic Lodge—and then you stop to check traffic from the opposite direction, because the highway narrows for a one-lane bridge as you cross the Downie River. This is the only place I know that Highway 49 goes to one lane, and the effect is absolutely charming.

But coming from the west has its allure as well. You will not have seen a business establishment for quite a while on Highway 49, and suddenly a roadside diner appears. (The food was very good on my visit.) Then you come to Cannon Point at a turn in the road, where a cannon believed to have been hauled from San Francisco sits. No one seems to be certain why it was brought to the community. It once was located near the Catholic church in town, where it was fired in celebration for the first time. Two gentlemen wanted to fire it again, but they were told not to because it needed to be cleaned after every firing. They set it off anyway, and both died from the experience. Celebration over.

After passing Cannon Point, you enter a town running at its own unhurried pace. When I was there one warm September weekday, the fire horn went off announcing high noon. A singer in front of a downtown bar, accompanying himself on guitar, stopped midline in "What a Day for a Daydream." Two men engaged in a spirited conversation outside the newspaper office halted. But the one man's dog tugged on his leash and gave out a soulful howl. When the siren ceased, the singer resumed from the same

Lizzie Campbell's headstone lies in the grass of the Downieville Cemetery.

Downieville's cemetery has dozens of exceptional grave markers of antiquity.

line, the spirited conversation was renewed, and the dog, exhausted from his howling protest, lay down on the sidewalk. Passersby, and I was one, avoided the dog by going into the street. The same thing probably happens in New York City all the time.

Downtown Downieville meets at Main and Commercial Streets. On the southeast corner stands the 1852 Craycroft Building, a brick and stone structure with an overhanging porch. A plaque states the building was famous for its seventy-foot-long basement bar, made from a single rip-sawn board.

Across the street on Main stands another excellent antique structure, the 1852 Mackerman Building. According to its historical marker, it has been a brewery, a drugstore, and a meat market. Currently it houses the state's oldest weekly newspaper, *The Mountain Messenger*. Its wooden false front is deceiving, because the building has three-foot-thick stone side walls and a four-foot-thick mud and brick ceiling.

Visible on a hill behind the Mackerman Building is the unusual steeple of the 1858 Immaculate Conception Catholic Church. To visit that church, follow Main Street east and immediately turn left onto School Street, which, not surprisingly, passes a gymnasium and a school. Continue around to the left, where you will see the church directly in front of you. This is the second building on the site; it replaced a church built in 1852 that burned in 1858. The front door handles have been removed. Worshippers and visitors access the very narrow church from the side, thus preventing people from entering and exiting the church amid Downieville's considerable "traffic."

The Immaculate Conception Catholic Church, built in 1858 after a fire destroyed the 1852 original, is one of the narrowest churches in the Northern Mines.

The former 1864 I.O.O.F. hall now serves as Downieville's library.

To reach the cemetery, only 0.6 of a mile from downtown, continue east on Main from Commercial and follow the road as it climbs through a neighborhood. Just after Oxford Mine Road goes left, veer left down onto Gold Bluff Road when Main drops to the right. The cemetery will be in view on your left. A sign states that this graveyard, dating from around 1876, was the second burial ground in Downieville. An earlier cemetery was being "disturbed by greedy miners," so the graves were disinterred and brought to this site. The most elaborate stone, for L. Byington (1820–1886), has an angel—one assumes St. Peter—writing a new name in the eternal book.

According to an historic marker, the 1852 Mackerman Building has been a brewery, a drug store, a meat market, and now is home to the *Mountain Messenger*.

For yet another Downieville historic spot, turn south from Main onto Nevada Street. You will cross a bridge and then come to a reproduction of the Sierra County Sheriff's Gallows, the site of the 1885 hanging of James O'Neill. That was the only time it was used, and that was the last legal execution in the county.

## WHEN YOU GO

*From North Bloomfield, head northeast out of town, following North Bloomfield Road for 1.4 miles. Turn left on Derbec Road and go 0.8 of a mile to Backbone Road and turn left. This will dovetail into Cruzon Grade Road and take you to North Columbia in 5.7 miles. If you didn't pass through North Columbia on your way to North Bloomfield (that would have happened if you took the shorter, more scenic route from Nevada City), be sure to take a look at the lovely former schoolhouse on your right as you enter town. By the time you reach North Columbia, Cruzon Grade Road will have dovetailed into Tyler Foote Crossing Road. Follow Tyler Foote Crossing Road from North Columbia for 4.6 miles to Oak Tree Road. Turn right and follow it for 2.6 miles to California Highway 49, which you will reach 0.2 of a mile north of the Gold Rush town of North San Juan. I suggest taking a small detour to explore that community.*

*Downieville is 28 miles northeast of North San Juan on California Highway 49.*

# SIERRA CITY

Major William Downie, for whom Downieville (see preceding entry) is named, claimed he was the first to find placer gold at this location in the winter of 1850–1851 but did not explore the area further. (It is worth noting, however, that Major Downie was a known exaggerator.) Two other citizens of Downieville, Philo A. Haven and Joseph Zumwalt, are usually given credit for the founding of Sierra City in 1850. (Zumwalt is also credited with bringing the mock-serious fraternal order E Clampus Vitus to the Gold Rush's Mokelumne Hill from his home in Missouri.) In that same year, miners began tunneling into the Sierra Buttes, which rise dramatically behind Sierra City, following a quartz ledge. In the winter of 1852–1853, those same buttes let loose an avalanche that destroyed the tiny community below. The town was not rebuilt until several years later when Ferdinand, Gustav, and Christian Reis reexamined old claims in the Sierra Buttes and found significant deposits. The town began anew.

Sierra City received its post office in 1864. Four years earlier, a mass of gold found in the Monumental Mine weighed 1,596 troy ounces, and another discovered in 1869 weighed even more—1,893 troy ounces. In 1878, the town of 400 citizens shipped $288,000 in gold via Wells Fargo. The total production of the Sierra City mines is estimated at $30 million.

## WALKING AND DRIVING AROUND SIERRA CITY

As you enter town coming from Downieville, you will pass the lovely 1867 Bigelow House, for sale at this writing, which has been both a bed and breakfast inn and a private residence since I first visited the town. The next attraction will be easy to miss, so watch for Cemetery Lane on your left. The graveyard stands on a steep hill and contains many ornate gravestones, shaded by oak and pine trees, for natives of England, Ireland, Scotland, France, Germany, Portugal, Italy, Sweden, Norway, Mexico, and the Azores.

As you return from the cemetery, before you reach the highway, turn left on Butte Street, which will take you past the St. Thomas Catholic Church.

The 1863 Masonic Hall stands on the corner of Butte and Main Streets in central Sierra City. Across the street on Butte is the 1879 Methodist Church, which has an unusual octagonal-roofed belfry.

The most impressive structure in town is on the north side of the street, east of the Masonic Hall. The two-story 1871 Busch and Heringlake Building was

The 1871 Busch and Heringlake Building has served multiple purposes, including the offices of both Wells Fargo and Western Union.

Sierra City's Methodist Church, built in 1879, has an unusual octagonal belfry.

A restored trestle leads ore cars to the huge mill at the Kentucky Mine, near Sierra City. The site is so complete that it is listed on the National Register of Historic Places.

built of local brick by August C. Busch and has been, according to a plaque, a residence, general store, and the offices of both Wells Fargo and Western Union.

At this writing the building is vacant, but it has recently been sold, so it may well be open for business when you visit Sierra City. Inside the building when I saw it in 1999 was a magnificent old safe with "A.C. Busch" written in ornate gold letters. The safe held miners' gold until it could be transferred to Wells Fargo, according to the then owner of the building. Incidentally, that same owner inquired of the St. Louis August Busch family to determine if Sierra City's August Busch was related to the famous brewer, but they replied he was not.

One mile east of town on Highway 49 is the turnoff to one of Sierra City's more productive gold mines, the Kentucky Mine, now known as the Sierra County Historical Park and Museum.

The Kentucky Mine began gold production in 1853. A five-stamp mill built in the 1860s was increased to ten stamps in 1888.

Emil Loeffler and his son Dutch are responsible for the preservation of the mine and mill. They reopened the mine in 1910 after it had been closed for years, even building a new mill largely out of salvaged equipment. That mill ran until 1944, when Dutch was killed in an accident in the mine. The mine was last worked in 1953.

The Sierra County Historical Society now operates the Kentucky Mine, which is open Wednesday through Sunday from Memorial Day weekend through Labor Day weekend. Its museum features mineral samples, mining and logging equipment, historical photographs, and Native American and Chinese artifacts.

The mill tour is a genuine treat. Most mills remaining in Gold Rush Country were stripped for salvage. The Kentucky Mill, however, is in virtually operable condition, making it extremely rare and well worth touring. The site is so complete that it was placed on the National Register of Historic Places. The reasonable admission price to the mill tour includes entrance to the museum.

## WHEN YOU GO

*Sierra City is 12.6 miles northeast of Downieville on California Highway 49.*

# JOHNSVILLE AND THE PLUMAS-EUREKA STATE PARK

Johnsville and the Plumas-Eureka State Park are interrelated and adjacent to each other. Since the mine predates the town, I suggest first visiting the state park, where the mine is located.

A group of nine prospectors first panned in Jamison Creek, which flows through the present-day state park, in May 1851. After incredibly rich primary deposits were found by two of their group on nearby Gold Mountain (now Eureka Peak), they and other friends formed the Eureka Company, the first California corporation created for the purpose of mining.

For the next twenty years, several small operations worked deposits with varying degrees of success. The name of the camp for the mines was Jamison City, which had a peak population of about two hundred.

The real bonanza came in 1872, when a British group, the Sierra Buttes Gold Mining Company Limited, bought up a series of claims, brought in the latest equipment, and consolidated the workings into one large operation. The Plumas-Eureka was born.

The headquarters and assay office of the Plumas-Eureka Mine still contains assaying equipment used to determine the value of the gold ore retrieved from the mine.

The Mohawk Mill of the Plumas-Eureka Mine contained sixty stamps. The din created by those stamps would have echoed throughout the area.

Blacksmith shop at the Plumas-Eureka Mine contains a forge, anvils, and assorted tools of the smithy's trade.

The mine had more than paid for itself within ten years and continued profitably for another twenty years before it was sold. The last good year was in 1897, although sporadic mining attempts were made into the 1940s. When production finally ceased, the mine had yielded more than $8 million in gold.

The Johnsville Hotel, no longer in service, has ornamental tin siding.

## WALKING AROUND PLUMAS-EUREKA STATE PARK

Begin your tour at the park headquarters and museum, housed in the former bunkhouse (open from Memorial Day weekend to Labor Day weekend, with limited hours year-round). A walking tour brochure takes you to the primary attraction, the huge 1878 Mohawk (later, the Plumas-Eureka) Mill, a sixty-stamp mill that is the equivalent of about a seven-story building. Other attractions include the mine office, a five-stamp mill, a stable, a fully functional blacksmith shop, and the Moriarity House, a miner's residence open for tours in the summer.

The same brochure will also lead you to the Jamison Mine, which is 1.7 miles southeast of the main area of the park at the end of Jamison Mine Road. There you will find several buildings of the Jamison Mine, which opened in the late 1880s. The first time I visited, I was reminded clearly about the presence of bears in the park. In the parking area for the Jamison Mine was an automobile that had been broken into and thoroughly, completely ransacked. What a surprise awaited the hikers who left food in that car!

The town of Johnsville, also clearly marked on the park brochure, was a company town erected in 1876 by the Sierra Buttes Company for their Plumas-Eureka Mine. Originally called Johnstown, it was named for William Johns, the well-respected manager of the Plumas-Eureka Mine. When a post office was granted in 1882, the name was changed to Johnsville.

The premier building is the 1908 two-story Johnsville Hotel, which features decorative tin siding. On the opposite side of the street stands the firehouse, rebuilt in 1967 to its 1908 appearance. All but a few of the town's residences are occupied, and most are nicely maintained.

Immediately north of the hotel is Church Street. Take Church east to the cemetery, which has an amazing variety of birthplace countries, considering its small size: natives of Greece, Ireland, Italy, Scotland, England, Switzerland, Austria, and Herzegovina are buried there. One notable grave is for Johnsville native John Redstreake (1911–1981), the "undefeated long-board snowshoe champion." The first organized races in the western hemisphere on skis, then called "snowshoes," were held in this area in 1861.

## WHEN YOU GO

*From the Kentucky Mine 1 mile east of Sierra City, return to California Highway 49 and turn left. In 4 miles, turn left at the junction with Forest Service Road 24, also known as the Gold Lake Forest Highway. After 14.3 miles of remarkably scenic driving, you will arrive at California Highway 89. Turn left. From there, drive north 2.7 miles through the delightful community of Graeagle to the intersection of California Highways 89 and 70. Turn left. In 0.6 of a mile, turn left again at County Road A14, Mohawk Highway Road, where a sign directs you to Plumas-Eureka State Park. In 0.6 of a mile, turn right onto Graeagle-Johnsville Road. The park headquarters is 4.5 miles up that road.*

*Important Note: This state park is the second in this book that was slated to close in 2012 due to budgetary shortfalls. If the park is barricaded so that you cannot see the buildings of the Mohawk Mine, I would have second thoughts about the journey from Sierra City to Johnsville (although the route is lovely). Johnsville is a minor site when separated from the state park. I definitely recommend going to the website given on page 13 to determine the status of this state park.*

# 3
# GHOSTS
## OF THE
# NORTH
# COUNTRY

GHOST TOWNS FAN OUT from Redding to the northwesternmost reaches of California. The area is rich in landscapes, featuring the lovely Trinity and Scott Rivers and, from a distance, magnificent Mount Shasta and Lassen Peak. The ghost towns are definitely enhanced by these surroundings and the scenic, twisting back roads that wind through the area. Take your time and enjoy the landscape. Despite the relatively rural nature of this chapter, all sites are on paved roads.

Incidentally, the last site in this chapter, Callahan, is about two-and-a-half hours away from Jacksonville, Oregon, a delightful former mining town that is close to three other ghost town sites in southwestern Oregon. Those towns are featured in my book *Ghost Towns of the Pacific Northwest*, forthcoming from Voyageur Press.

The Costco of its time, Shasta's Bull, Baker & Co. was the largest wholesaler in Northern California.

The Masonic section of the Weaverville Cemetery contains many headstones of antiquity.

# SHASTA

Shasta is the principal reminder in northern California that gold was not found solely in the Mother Lode and the Northern Mines. The first gold discovery in Shasta County was made in March 1848 by Major Pierson B. Reading, who, with the help of Indians, washed out about $800 per day from placers along Clear Creek. The tent city that grew was originally called Reading's Diggings or Reading's Springs. The name was changed to Shasta City in 1850, and when the post office was established a year later, the name was shortened to Shasta, a corruption of the name of an Indian tribe.

Shasta became an important metropolis not only for its own gold but also because the town became the gateway both to gold-rich Trinity County and to the rapidly opening Oregon frontier. The main street became lined with businesses to outfit expeditions and crowded with mule trains to carry the goods across the rugged trails that led west and north.

In 1853, fire swept through town. To avoid a recurrence, merchants rebuilt with brick, giving Shasta the distinction of having the longest row of brick buildings in California at that time. The permanence of the new business district indicated the optimism that the merchants felt for Shasta's future, and for a time it was justified.

The 1855–56 Litsch Store and Bakery, located on the east end of Shasta, contains scores of new-old-stock items once sold there.

Most of the brick buildings in Shasta are mere shells, but they still have the look of permanence of the Gold Rush Country, far to the south.

At their peak, the mines in Trinity and Siskiyou Counties were producing as much as $100,000 in ore per week, much of it freighted through town. During the winter of 1854–55, an estimated 1,876 mules were packing supplies through Shasta. One mule reportedly carried a 352-pound safe from Shasta to Weaverville and then proceeded to lie down and die.

Shasta itself began to lie down and die in 1886, when the Central Pacific Railroad connecting San Francisco and Portland bypassed the town in favor of nearby Reading (later spelled "Redding" for B. B. Redding, a railroad employee).

## WALKING AND DRIVING AROUND SHASTA

Shasta is now a California State Historic Park. Its street of brick buildings is still impressive, even though many have been reduced to mere walls and foundations. Start your visit at the former Shasta County Courthouse on the north side of the street (see page 99).

East of the courthouse stands the 1853 Masonic Lodge, whose charter was brought westward by Peter Lassen, for whom Lassen Peak is named.

The 1855–56 Litsch Store and Bakery, located on the east end of Shasta, contains scores of new-old-stock items once sold there. Some of the canned goods are reproductions, but a park employee assured me that the champagne, wine, and liquor bottles were genuine and had never been opened. They were also inconveniently out of reach. Shasta's two cemeteries are worth seeking out. The closer, behind the courthouse along Trinity Alley, contains many stones from the 1850s. The tombstone for Hugh H. Burns, who died in 1853, reads: "Killed by Indians on Stillwater." To reach the second, an 1864 I.O.O.F. cemetery now maintained by the Masons, head east on California Highway 299 toward Redding, turn right on Red Bluff Road, go past the Shasta School, and turn right onto Mule Town Road. The cemetery will be on your left, a half mile from the main highway.

One more grave deserves your inspection. Less than a mile west of Shasta is a sign leading you to the grave site of Elchanan Broinshstein (Charles Brownstein), who died in 1864 at only seven months. His parents brought his body from Red Bluff to be buried in Shasta's Jewish Cemetery. The original headstone and forgotten cemetery were discovered in 1923 by highway engineers. The highway was rerouted to avoid the graveyard.

## WHEN YOU GO

*Shasta is 4 miles west of Redding on California Highway 299. Note: Do not confuse this site with the towns of Shasta Lake, 8 miles north of Redding on Interstate 5, or Mount Shasta, 54 miles north of Shasta Lake on Interstate 5.*

***Important Note:*** *This state park is the third in this book that was slated to close in 2012 due to budgetary shortfalls. What that likely means is that the courthouse/museum and the Litsch Store would be closed, but you can certainly see the buildings and ruins on both sides of the highway. I recommend going to the website given on page 13 to determine the status of this state park.*

## Shasta Courthouse Museum

The Shasta County Courthouse Museum is located inside the county's original courthouse. Erected in 1855, the handsome brick structure served in that capacity from 1862 until 1888, when Shasta lost the county seat to Redding.

In addition to a completely restored courtroom, the museum features a variety of Gold Rush–era memorabilia, including collections of rifles, revolvers, and pocket watches. I found a display of implements of the Chinese particularly interesting, especially when you combine this museum with the Joss House State Park in Weaverville (see page 102).

A unique feature of the museum is the Boggs Collection, an array of California art depicting life in the state between 1850 and 1950. The paintings were collected by Mae Helene Bacon Boggs, who arrived in Shasta at age eight in 1871. She was also a key person in the creation of Shasta State Historic Park by helping to preserve the land that eventually was donated for the park.

The downstairs of the courthouse contains a four-cell jail and a doorway out to a backyard gallows.

# FRENCH GULCH

French miners exploring a gulch in 1849 or 1850 found significant gold deposits, and when a post office was granted in 1856, it honored its earliest pioneers and the location of their discovery: French Gulch.

From two water-driven stamp mills in 1851, the area grew in production to require eleven mills by 1900. The scurrying for gold grew to such a pace that in 1852 the Shasta *Courier* reported that in French Gulch "such rich diggings have been struck that miners are tearing down their houses to pursue the leads which run under them." Gold fever eventually cooled, but not before the mines produced almost $28 million in gold.

## WALKING AND DRIVING AROUND FRENCH GULCH

The most attractive building in town today is the French Gulch Hotel and Dining Room, built in 1885 by Irishman Richard H. Feeney. The bar was fashioned in England, sent around Cape Horn to San Francisco, and carted overland to French Gulch.

Across the street is the 1854 rock and mud Fox Store, which for most of its history was the E. Franck and Co. Store. Up the street on my earlier visits was

The French Gulch Hotel and Dining Room remains the center of the action in this small community.

a large, two-story 1906 I.O.O.F. Hall, but it was a casualty of the French Fire, which swept around and through French Gulch in August 2004. A small, false-front, wooden building stands in its place. North of that structure stand several attractive, well-kept residences.

What was French Gulch's most photographed building, the lovely 1898 St. Rose's Catholic Church, was a charred ruin in 1999, the target of arsonists. When I returned in 2011, I hoped to find it rebuilt, but the lot is still vacant.

French Gulch features two cemeteries. The trail to the smaller Catholic cemetery, which begins on the southwest corner of French Gulch Road and Main Street, across Main from the now-missing church, was posted against trespassing in 1999 and again in 2011. The trail is now overgrown. Perhaps the sign was a necessary step, because when I visited in the early 1980s, I found a dozen monuments that had been systematically toppled.

To reach the public cemetery, drive north through town and turn west on Niagara Street. There you will find at least a dozen members of the Franck family, eight of whom are inscribed on one lovely, elaborate headstone. Two of those names are F. A. and E. E. Franck, two of the founders of the E. Franck and Co. Store. Incidentally, I did not find one obviously French name in either French Gulch cemetery.

This ornate marble monument, with a kind of urn atop it, names eight members of the Franck family. Two of them, F. A. and E. E. Franck, were the founders of the E. Franck and Co. Store, which still stands across the road from the French Gulch Hotel and Dining Room. At this writing, however, it no longer serves as a store.

## WHEN YOU GO

*From Shasta State Park, drive 12.1 miles west on California Highway 299 to Trinity Mountain Road, the turnoff to French Gulch. French Gulch is 2.9 miles north.*

# WEAVERVILLE

Weaverville is more alive than any other site in this chapter. You will pass several blocks of modern America before you enter Weaverville's nineteenth-century historic district, but, once there, you will be charmed.

In 1850 George Weaver built a cabin at this spot, and within two years Weaverville had forty buildings and a population of 1,200. By 1854 the town had its first newspaper, and in 1858 a telegraph line linked the town to the outside world. Downtown Weaverville featured twenty-one brick buildings by 1859, nineteen of which still stand today.

Early Weaverville was fragmented into many ethnic sections, including a Chinatown. Most mining camps attempted to restrict mining by Chinese with ownership laws, excessive taxes, and officially or unofficially sanctioned violence. For example, in Shasta (the first entry in this chapter), the Chinese were summarily expelled in 1856. Weaverville was an exception. Although prejudice no doubt existed in the young camp, it was not town policy. As a result, Chinese began to settle there in great numbers, at one point constituting about half the population.

## WALKING AND DRIVING AROUND WEAVERVILLE

By 1862 Weaverville had twenty-eight saloons, and one visitor complained that liquor, gambling, and fighting were the favorite pastimes of the citizenry. But Weaverville also had its sophisticated side as well, best exemplified today by the stately buildings that remain in the central business district. A good example is the 1856 Trinity County Courthouse, at Court and Main Streets. The building, constructed by Henry Hocker, originally served as a hotel, store, and saloon.

Three two-story buildings on Main Street demonstrate a Weaverville architectural curiosity: each structure has an ornate spiral staircase leading from the sidewalk to the second floor. Although the buildings were two-story, the ownership of the two floors was separate, necessitating two independent entrances. A good illustration of this is the 1856 Old Ryans Store and, above it, the I.O.O.F. Hall.

The most elegant and unusual structure in town is due to the Chinese. Because of their acceptance in the community, they built a graceful Taoist temple in 1853. When that one burned, they built another in 1874 and named it Won Lim Miao, "The Temple Amongst the Forest Beneath the Clouds." Nonpractitioners know the lovely building on Main Street as the Weaverville

The building currently housing Olson Stoneware is one of three two-story structures on Weaverville's Main Street demonstrating an architectural oddity: each building has a spiral staircase leading from the sidewalk to the second story. Although the structures had two floors, each floor had a separate owner, necessitating two independent entrances.

Joss House. It is now a state historic park even as it continues to serve as an active temple. To view the ornate interior of the temple, take an informative and inexpensive thirty-minute tour.

Another worthwhile place to visit is the J. J. Jackson Memorial Museum, located south of the Joss House on Main Street. The museum features era clothing, bottles, and apothecary paraphernalia, as well as samples of Native American crafts and ranching and mining memorabilia. In the basement are two cells from the 1880s that stood in the Trinity County Courthouse until 1968. Peer inside to see the interesting prisoners' graffiti and drawings adorning the walls.

This two-story brick building stands directly across from the Olsen Stoneware store. Notice that its spiral staircase stands in the middle of the building.

Weaverville has two cemeteries. The larger is located on Oregon Street behind the Joss House. There you will find an unusually large number of elaborate antique stones among more modern ones. The oldest stone I found dated from 1859.

To visit the Catholic cemetery, return to Main Street. Go west to Court, turn right, and turn right again in two blocks at the Catholic church sign. This cemetery is adjacent to the lovely 1924 St. Patrick's Church, the fourth such building on the site. The previous three burned, but the present one closely resembles the others, the first of which dated from 1853. One prominent citizen buried there is Henry Hocker (1826–1882), builder of the courthouse.

Won Lim Miao, "The Temple Amongst the Forest Beneath the Clouds," is the primary attraction of the Weaverville Joss House State Park even as it continues to serve as an active temple.

The Trinity County Courthouse, still in use, was built in 1856, originally serving as a hotel, store, and saloon.

This double headstone for the children of John D. Munster is very unusual, because ordinarily such a monument would be for infants or at least very young children. This is the first I have ever seen in which the siblings were adults: Emma was 29 when she died, and John was 27. They were born three years apart, but they died within a year of each other. Notice that there is no mention of their mother on the headstone.

At one time, Weaverville had three Chinese cemeteries, but no longer, despite the large Chinese population. For an explanation of this oddity, see the Chinese Camp entry in Chapter 1 (page 56).

West of Weaverville is evidence of the mining that once enveloped the area. The La Grange Mine, 3.7 miles from town on California Highway 299, was the world's largest hydraulic mine, with more than one hundred million yards of gravel hosed down from the hillside to release about $3.5 million in gold. A hydraulic monitor, a kind of water cannon, stands next to the highway. You can see, across the canyon and in the fragile vegetation behind you, the environmental havoc the process caused. For a more detailed explanation on hydraulicking, see the entry for North Bloomfield and Malakoff Diggins State Park (page 72). As you head toward Helena, the next entry in this chapter, you will actually be driving *inside a mine*, as implausible as that seems.

## WHEN YOU GO

*Weaverville is 44 miles northwest of Redding and 29 miles northwest of the turnoff to French Gulch on California Highway 299.*

***Important Note:*** *The Joss House State Park is the fourth in this book that was slated to close in 2012 due to budgetary shortfalls. That has little effect on touring Weaverville itself, and you can get an excellent view of the exterior of the Joss House on your way up to the public cemetery. But the interior of the temple is spectacular, so I do hope you will be able to see it. I recommend going to the website given on page 13 to determine the status of this state park.*

# HELENA

Helena came as a delightful surprise for me. On my first visit, the afternoon light gave Helena's brick buildings a warm look, and absolutely no one was there to disturb the serenity of the spot. The town features about a half dozen buildings under roof, most sheltered by drooping trees or partially obscured by shrubs.

The first mining camp in the area was lightheartedly called Bagdad because of its exotic and international nature: *Trinity County Historic Sites* reports that "ladies of accommodation" who settled there came from various countries. A Bagdad miner described them as "mademoiselles, señoritas, and jungfraus." Bagdad was on the east side of the North Fork of the Trinity River. On the west side another camp grew, known simply as North Fork.

John Meckel and his younger brother Christian came to North Fork in 1853 and opened a general merchandise and pack train business. Two years later Harmon Schlomer arrived and opened a blacksmith shop and eventually built a toll bridge and a three-story brick building. The history of North Fork essentially became the history of the Meckel and Schlomer families. Their stories became intertwined when John Meckel and Harm Schlomer married sisters.

A ghostly two-story clapboard residence stands northwest of the main structures in Helena.

The Schlomer Clubhouse and Sleeping Quarters is located between the two brick buildings in Helena.

In 1870 Christian Meckel went to Germany and returned with a bride, Helena. In 1891, the town's post office was changed in her honor and to avoid confusion with another North Fork in California. By then, the men of Helena were only part-time miners, with most augmenting their incomes as farmers. Helena, with its orchards, grape arbors, and clear rivers, became a favorite Sunday-outing destination for young men and women from Weaverville.

## WALKING AND DRIVING AROUND HELENA

As you enter Helena today, the first building you will notice is a moody, red brick, three-story edifice erected by Harm Schlomer in 1859. In 1861 the Schlomers lived on the top two floors and had a saloon in the basement. The building later became known as The Brewery, even though beer was actually brought from Weaverville. Over the years the building served as a schoolhouse, the site of an occasional Catholic mass, and a combination office and residence.

Up the road stands a wooden building that was the Schlomer Clubhouse and Sleeping Quarters. Across the street is another sturdy brick building, the 1858 Meckel Brothers General Merchandise, which also housed the post office. The Brewery and the Meckel Brothers Store are the only two surviving historic brick structures in Trinity County not in Weaverville.

Harm Schlomer constructed this three-story brick structure in Helena in 1859. It served as a residence and a saloon and even was pressed into service as a schoolhouse.

Across the street to the west is Harm Schlomer's wooden feed store and stable, and beyond is a deteriorating residence. Down the road and across the street from that residence is a large chimney of a house that no longer stands.

The Helena Cemetery stands southeast of town. Return to California Highway 299, cross the bridge going east, and stop to read the marker about Bagdad. Immediately beyond that marker, turn left from the highway. That road takes you in a few yards to what is now called the Trinity County Cemetery.

There are ten marked graves of the pioneer Schlomer family, including H. Harmon K. Schlomer (1825–1898).

Most of the Meckel family members left Helena and moved to Weaverville, where several are buried in both the public and Catholic cemeteries. Only Edna Meckel (1883–1946) has a marker in the Helena Cemetery.

## WHEN YOU GO

*From Weaverville, drive 14.7 miles west on California Highway 299. Turn right on East Fork Road and proceed 0.3 of a mile to Helena.*

# CALLAHAN

Callahan, located at the south end of Scott Valley at the junction of the east and south forks of the Scott River, was named for M. B. Callahan, who built the site's first cabin in 1851 and opened a hotel the following year. He sold the hotel and left the area in 1855, but by 1857 the Callahan Ranch Hotel was serving as a stage station—the first in Siskiyou County—for the California and Oregon Stage Company, whose stages traversed a toll road from Shasta through Callahan and on to Yreka. When the post office opened in 1858, it was for Callahans Ranch, a name shortened to Callahan in 1892. The stage route became obsolete in 1887 when the Central Pacific Railroad was completed between San Francisco and Portland. The gold deposits that first brought people to the valley played out in the 1890s, although dredging operations continued into the 1950s. Dredging evidence extends for several miles north of Callahan.

The 1854 Callahan Ranch Hotel, which closed in the 1930s, is being restored at this writing.

## WALKING AND DRIVING AROUND CALLAHAN

If you are coming from Weaverville, on your right as you enter Callahan is the town's most photogenic building, the wood-frame, two-story 1854 Callahan Ranch Hotel, which closed in the 1930s. On my visit in 2011, the long-vacant building was undergoing extensive renovation.

Across the street are three connected commercial buildings. On the south end is the Callahan Emporium, which opened in the early days of the twentieth century. In the middle is the 1890, two-story, cut-stone A. H. Denny Building. Next to it is the Mount of Bolivar Grange (Mount Bolivar is south of Callahan).

Next door to the Callahan Ranch Hotel stands the two-story Farringtons Hotel, which operated from 1867 until 1925. When I visited in the 1980s and mid-1990s, part of the building was open for groceries and gasoline, with the

This two-story residence in Callahan has lost its southeastern wing, but it does have a modern protective metal roof.

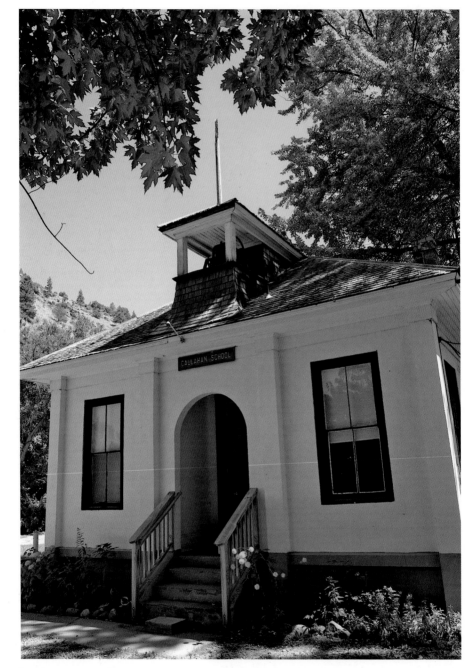

The former Callahan School, now a private residence, still has its bell in the belfry.

Farrington family still running the business. When I returned in 1999, a sign on the door announced, "After 130 years of continued service to the community of Callahan, the Farrington family is no longer in business. . . . Thank you for your business and your friendship through the years." In 2011, the large, long building was unoccupied.

A driveway between the Callahan Ranch Hotel and Farringtons takes you to the old Callahan School, now a private residence. A sizable, two-story residence, which has lost one of its wings, stands behind Farringtons.

To visit Callahan's cemeteries, turn west immediately south of the Emporium. South Fork Road takes you past the 1894 community church, originally the Congregational church. Land for the church was donated by A. H. Denny in memory of his wife, Elisa, who had hoped the town would someday have a Protestant church. The building has an unusual, attractive wave pattern in its shingled siding.

Beyond the community church is a large boulder on the left side of the road with an inserted plaque that denotes the site of Scott Valley's first Catholic church, erected in about 1858. Just beyond that marker is Callahan's Protestant Cemetery. There you will see headstones for several members of the Denny family, including Elisa Webber Denny, who died in 1881 at age thirty-nine. Several markers remind us that the name of the town has changed slightly: headstones have the town as "Callahans," "Callahan's," and "Callahan."

A short distance south is the Catholic cemetery, which has a poignant double marker for James and Fidelia Littlefield, both of whom died, at ages eight and six, respectively, on December 15, 1877. One can almost hear their parents' grief with the epitaph: "Our Children—Rest Beloved Ones Rest." What a mournful Christmas that must have been ten days later.

## WHEN YOU GO

*Callahan is 68 miles north of Weaverville on California Highway 3.*

# 4
# GHOSTS
## O F
# SAN FRANCISCO
# BAY

GHOST TOWN ENTHUSIASTS usually visit the sights of the San Francisco Bay area as a separate activity from ghost towning. But you may be surprised to know that five ghosts are located close to San Francisco.

This is the only chapter in the book to cover sites located near a large body of water, which introduces a new kind of "ghost": the ghost fort. Three forts in this chapter were erected to protect American interests from foreign attack.

Unlike the other chapters of this book, not one site in this chapter existed because of mining. The premier attraction is Alcatraz, originally a military stronghold and later a famous prison—but also a ghost town as well. Angel Island offers two ghostly forts in a stunningly beautiful, peaceful setting. Fort Point stands underneath the Golden Gate Bridge and remains one of the foremost examples of granite stone-crafting and brick masonry-building in the United States. China Camp, now a state park, is a ghost fishing village and a reminder that injustices done to the Chinese were not confined to the Mother Lode. And, finally, the tiny river delta town of Locke is a unique former agricultural community also settled by the Chinese.

The East side of Locke's Main Street's with its seemingly rickety two-story combination commercial and residential buildings.

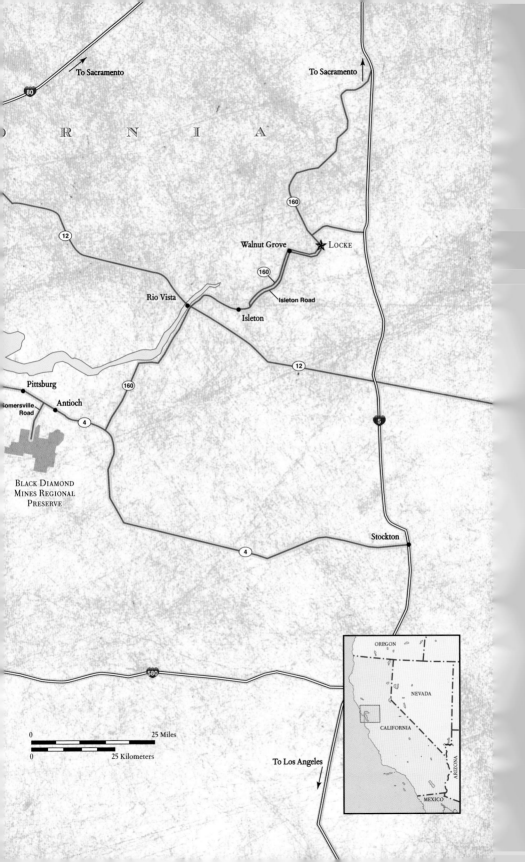

# ALCATRAZ

Alcatraz was "a small town with a big jail," according to former head guard Philip Bergen. In addition to its "big jail," Alcatraz was home to about 300 civilians who shopped in the small store, received mail at the post office, and attended events in a social hall that featured a bowling alley. Among those civilians were sixty to eighty children who played on a concrete playground (no cap pistols or rubber knives, however) and were ferried daily to school in San Francisco, a mere one-and-a-quarter miles away. Bergen's daughter remembers fondly, "It was a great place to grow up. . . . There were parties for kids, formal dances for the teens. We were within steps of the prison, but no one locked their doors."

Those children and their parents have gone, and Alcatraz is now a small *ghost* town with a big *ghost* jail. It is also one of the West's most fascinating places to visit.

Isla de Alcatraces (Spanish for "Pelican Island") was the name bestowed in 1775 on what is now known as Yerba Buena Island in San Francisco Bay. The name was transferred to the place now popularly called "The Rock" in 1826.

The Gold Rush made Alcatraz important. The amazing Mother Lode brought hundreds of ships with tens of thousands of people to San Francisco through the Golden Gate, and Alcatraz had the Pacific Coast's first lighthouse, built in 1854, to usher them in safely. When the Civil War broke out, San Francisco's enormous gold supply (and silver supply from Nevada's Comstock Lode) tempted the Confederacy, but by that time Alcatraz also was the Pacific Coast's first permanent military outpost, with 111 cannons and rows of gun emplacements. The strength of Alcatraz and other fortifications deterred the Confederacy, and not one shot was fired from the battlements. (That might have been fortunate, because during an 1876 centennial celebration, a ship was towed into range for Alcatraz's mighty cannons to obliterate. They failed.)

In addition to its navigational and strategic importance, Alcatraz has a long history as a prison. As early as 1859, it was an army disciplinary barracks. During the Civil War, it housed deserters and other military miscreants along with citizens accused of treason and the crew of a Confederate privateer. In the late 1800s, it held prisoners from various Indian wars, including members of the Modoc, Apache, and Hopi tribes. After the 1906 San Francisco earthquake, the island housed 106 of the city's inmates, as its jail was in ruins.

In 1907 Alcatraz was deemed no longer necessary for defense, and it was converted to a full-time military prison. Construction began in 1908 on the huge

Built by the army in the 1920s on top of the Alcatraz Island guardhouse and sally port, this building has always been known as "The Chapel," although there is no record of its ever being used for that purpose. Its principal function during both military and prison duty was as a quarters for single men, although it served for a short time, during the military phase, as a schoolhouse.

cell house that still dominates the island, a structure that was at the time the world's largest steel-reinforced concrete building. It was designed so cells had neither an outside wall nor an outside ceiling—escaping one's cell would still leave the inmate within the building's walls. The prisoners who helped construct the cell house were its first occupants when it was completed in 1912.

The Parade Ground stands on the south end of Alcatraz. It was here that the children of guards played. The overgrown piles of rubble in the center and right are all that is left of the family housing, leveled in 1972. In the background is San Francisco, with the Bay Bridge extending toward Oakland.

The federal penitentiary that gave the island its notoriety was opened in 1934 as a place to house inmates whose behavior at other federal prisons made them particular risks. Alcatraz was for many of them the end of the prison line. Here, on a chilly, desolate battleship of land, inmates were scrutinized by one staff member for every three prisoners (as opposed to the normal federal ratio of one to ten) and counted as often as fourteen times daily. Among the most infamous were Al Capone, "Machine Gun" Kelly, and Robert Stroud, the "Bird Man of Alcatraz," who in fact had birds at Leavenworth penitentiary, but not at Alcatraz.

The food was good and prisoners were not mistreated physically, despite Hollywood's various depictions. But there was one cruel punishment: the proximity of the lights and sounds of San Francisco. As one inmate reported, "There was never a day when you couldn't see what you were losing." On New Year's Eve, it was said that inmates could even hear champagne corks popping at shoreline clubs.

The average stay at Alcatraz was from eight to ten years; the longest was three months short of twenty-eight years, which was virtually the length of time the prison was in service. It closed in 1963 because buildings were deteriorating and the prison was overly expensive to run. Of the 1,545 men who did time over those twenty-nine years, eight were murdered, five committed suicide, seven were killed attempting to escape, and two were eventually executed at the prison at San Quentin for killing two Alcatraz guards. No successful escape is known, although five inmates were presumed drowned in San Francisco Bay. One inmate in 1962 actually made it to rocks near the Golden Gate Bridge, but he was too exhausted to climb to dry land and was apprehended.

After Alcatraz's closing in 1963, the island was uninhabited, except for a caretaker, until November 1969, when fourteen Native American students invaded the island. Eventually a group calling itself the "Indians of All Tribes" claimed possession of Alcatraz under a Sioux treaty of 1868 guaranteeing that abandoned federal lands would revert to Indians. The occupiers sardonically claimed that the island would be an ideal place for Indians since it was isolated from modern facilities, had inadequate sanitation, no running water, high unemployment, and no educational facilities. It was also a place where the population had always been held as prisoners and kept dependent upon others. The federal authorities were not amused and eventually cut off electricity and water supplies before evicting the Indians in June 1971.

Scars of that occupation remain on Alcatraz. A fire on June 2, 1970, destroyed the lighthouse keeper's home, the once-lovely warden's residence, and the Post Exchange.

## WALKING AROUND ALCATRAZ

I suggest, when you arrive at Alcatraz, to try to forget the prison's cinematic portrayals and see it for what it was, because former inmate Jim Quillan worries that movies, books, and legends have glorified the prison. He reminds us that Alcatraz was "about isolation, sadness, anger, and death." Glenn Williams, another inmate, says simply: "This was a horrible, horrible place."

Understanding Alcatraz's reality is much easier if you do two things: buy an inexpensive brochure detailing the layout of the island and take the excellent recorded tour of the cell house. The tour is narrated by former guards and inmates and features the sounds of clanging doors and the echoes of men's voices. The effect is mesmerizing. But you will not be alone. Expect crowds along this tour: about 1.4 million visitors flock to Alcatraz annually, which is almost four thousand people per day. If you are there during the peak seasons, you will have much more company than that.

After the headphone tour, be sure to walk everywhere you are permitted to go. Make a thorough exploration of corridors and walking paths, and be certain to visit the Recreation Yard. From there you can see the prisoners' views of the Bay Area, so close but so distant. Along one wall of the yard is a small door that

The Recreation Yard, adjacent to the Cell House, has been used in several motion pictures about life on Alcatraz.

led to the prison workshops and laundry. At that entrance was a metal detector through which inmates returning from work would have to pass. The convicts had a perfect name for it: The Mechanical Stool Pigeon.

Most of the ghost prison is still standing, but little of the ghost town. On the island's southeast end, you can look down to a large parade ground (on an earlier visit in 2000, I saw hundreds of seagulls in formation) that served as the playground for the town's children. Here is a memory from Jolene Babyak, who grew up on the island: "This two-acre slab of concrete was our batting field, our skating rink, our tennis court, our touch football gridiron. It was a cement [sic] prairie on which the winds played furiously." Adjacent to that space is the rubble of the families' apartments, which were bulldozed in 1972. Newly arrived families lived in the former 1905–06 military barracks, the four-story building standing adjacent to the wharf where your ferry docked. It was converted into apartments, but it was definitely the least desirable place to live. One new guard reported, "My wife cried when I showed it to her the first time. Then a fellow resigned and we had a real nice apartment. You got your apartment furnished with utilities paid for $25 a month. There's no way you could beat that. Not in San Francisco."

Opposite page: The residence for the warden at Alcatraz was burned during the Native American occupation in 1970. It was built in the 1920s for the commander of the military prison.

## WHEN YOU GO

*Ferries leave San Francisco's Fisherman's Wharf (Pier 33) to Alcatraz Island on a frequent basis, but advance reservations are essential. Incidentally, neither food nor drink is sold on the island.*

# ANGEL ISLAND

Angel Island offers one of the premier day trips of the Bay Area. Visitors leave behind the human tumult and San Francisco's exorbitantly priced real estate to discover solitude, relaxation, and, yes, even ghost towns—or at least ghost forts.

Isla de Los Angeles was named in 1775 by Lt. Juan Manuel de Ayala, commander of the packet *San Carlos*, which anchored in the cove that now bears Ayala's name. Angel Island has been the site of Indian villages, a Spanish rancho, a hangout for thieves and a dueling ground, a Civil War fortification, a sandstone quarry, a military detention center, a quarantine station, an army base, an immigration facility, and even a Nike missile base. Remains of several of these deployments stand on the island today, creating a day-long adventure for naturalists, photographers, and ghost town enthusiasts.

## HIKING, CYCLING, OR RIDING THE TRAM OR A SEGWAY ON ANGEL ISLAND

You will dock at Ayala Cove, which, beginning in 1891, housed a quarantine station where foreign ships were fumigated and possibly contagious immigrants were isolated. A two-story attendants' quarters from that era now houses a museum.

A tram that circumnavigates the island leaves from Ayala Cove, and I took it once simply to be able to report about it. If, however, you want more than a cursory glance at the highlights of the island, I cannot recommend it. It stops for only a

Camp Reynolds's warehouse, with its old wharf pilings rotting in San Francisco Bay, stands at the base of the parade ground.

The Artillery Barracks, seen in both a front and back view, housed 600 soldiers at Fort McDowell's military induction center.

Camp Reynolds's officers quarters—boarded up, grayish-white, two-story wooden residences—appear to be standing at frozen attention beside the parade ground on Angel Island.

few minutes at the island's major attractions, which would be very frustrating for a photographer, for example. But it certainly is the easiest way to enjoy the island and the only option for some. A newer way to go is a Segway tour, but, again, you cannot venture out on your own or set your own timetable.

If you really desire to investigate Angel Island, I recommend walking or, as I did on two visits, riding a mountain bicycle. These are not easy options, as the perimeter road of the island is five miles around, and it is very hilly in places. In addition, to visit the great ghost forts you must descend from the perimeter road almost to the shoreline and then, alas, venture back up. This is much more than a mere walk or ride in the park. I spent more than four hours on my first visit, exploring everything I could find. Almost thirty years later, on my third visit, I spent about three hours and was certainly reminded that I was almost thirty years older. With jogs down to the attractions and various side routes, I estimate I rode about seven miles. You can bring your own bike or rent one on the island. You must pay attention to the time of day, as you don't want to miss that last ferry.

Your first ghost fort is southwest of Ayala Cove. Camp Reynolds was established in 1863 to repel a potential Confederate attack on San Francisco and its enormous gold and silver supply. More than a dozen buildings stand near a parade ground sloping toward the bay. Most of the structures are officers' quarters—boarded-up, two-story

wooden residences that appear to be standing at frozen attention beside the parade ground. Near the shore stands a large brick warehouse built in 1909 that housed camp supplies and ordnance for the island's gun emplacements. The Commanding Officer's Quarters, standing at the top of the parade ground, is occasionally open for tours.

On the southeast end of Angel Island are the considerable remains of Fort McDowell. Begun in 1899 as a detainment facility for soldiers returning from the Spanish-American War who had been exposed to contagious diseases, the facility became known as Fort McDowell two years later when it became a discharge center for the same war. In 1910, Fort McDowell was greatly enlarged and became a military induction center. During World War II, the fort was a crucial point of embarkation for troops bound for the Pacific.

Most of Fort McDowell's buildings date from the 1910 enlargement. You will enter along Officers' Row, a stately procession of two-story, red-tile-roofed residences, some of which house park employees. The major structures of Fort McDowell are down the road: a chapel, a combination mess hall and gymnasium, a supply store, artillery headquarters, an administration building, and a hulking 600-man barracks.

Ghost town enthusiasts are accustomed to the partial remnants of buildings that were flimsy when built and meant to last only for a bonanza's duration. Fort McDowell is different. It looks as if it could withstand anything on the Richter scale that San Francisco could take.

Angel Island's Fort McDowell features an Officers' Row of elegant, sturdy residences topped with mission tile roofs.

On the north side of Angel Island is the least ghostly of the installations on the island, an immigration station that began operation in 1905. Unlike New York's Ellis Island, this facility was not built to welcome and process immigrants but rather to attempt to exclude them, as most arriving at the station were Chinese during a period of anti-Asian sentiment, although many other nationalities also were processed there, such as Mexicans, Latin and South Americans, Australians, New Zealanders, and Canadians. Immediately prior to World War II, more than 8,000 Jewish and Russian immigrants arrived, spurred to action by the rise of Nazism. But the primary would-be immigrants were Chinese, and only those who could prove they had relatives in this country could enter, a process made trickier when the 1906 earthquake and subsequent fire destroyed immigration records. The station closed in 1940. The main attraction is the barracks building, which houses an informative museum with often touching displays, such as mournful, desperate poems carved into the walls by detainees. Not far from the barracks is a marker in memory of the 175,000 Chinese who were detained here.

## WHEN YOU GO

*Visit Angel Island by ferry from San Francisco or Tiburon, or by private boat. Ferry res-
ervations are recommended, especially on holidays or summer weekends.*

# FORT POINT

San Francisco is filled with iconic images that tourists flock to see: the Golden Gate Bridge, cable cars, Coit Tower, the Transamerica Pyramid, Fisherman's Wharf, and many others. Yet nestled beneath that first icon, overlooked by most tourists, is one of the truly magnificent forts in American history.

Fort Point was erected between 1853 and 1861 as one of a series of planned fortresses to protect San Francisco Bay. As mentioned in the Alcatraz entry, enormous amounts of gold and silver were coming out of, first, the California Gold Rush, and, later, Nevada's silver Comstock Lode. The enemy that could capture even a portion of this wealth would have secured a bounty indeed. Fort Point was completed just as the Civil War commenced, and the Confederacy would have dearly liked to interrupt the supply of riches that was bankrolling the Union side. Their inability to do so was one of the circumstances that doomed the South to defeat.

Fort Point was built in the style of classic nineteenth-century American forts, like Fort Sumter and others on the Atlantic and Gulf Coasts. It was the only such fortification ever built on the Pacific shore. It consisted of beautifully sculpted granite and masterfully crafted brick masonry constructed so that the lowest bank of cannons could fire at water's level, aiming at ships' hulls, even utilizing the water to ricochet rounds to strike the enemy. The fort was protected, as were the forts in the eastern United States, by seven-foot-thick walls and multitiered casements (three in number at Fort Point), each of which would contain batteries of artillery. The challenges of constructing Fort Point were particularly daunting because it was constantly battered by the severe storms of the Pacific Ocean. By 1860, the fort had been completed to the top, or barbette, level, with the capability of holding 141 cannons, although it never exceeded 102 guns.

Although Fort Point (along with Alcatraz and Angel Island's Camp Reynolds) never fired a hostile shot during the Civil War, it served as a strong deterrent. But the success of enemy artillery upon the forts of similar masonry construction on the Atlantic Coast during that war convinced the United States Army that the forts were no longer strategically useful. Instead, it was determined that earthworks batteries were more effective at withstanding assault, along with being easier, faster, and less expensive to build. Fort Point was never fully occupied again. It was used in the 1920s to house unmarried officers at the nearby Presidio, as well as serving as facilities for military trade schools.

Fort Point could have vanished in the 1930s. The original plans for the Golden Gate Bridge proposed the demolition of the great fort, but Chief Engineer Joseph Strauss recognized the historic value of preserving the only fort of its kind on the Pacific Coast and so erected a special arch over the fort to protect it during the bridge's construction. In fact, the fort became the headquarters for the builders of the bridge.

Fort Point came into service again during World War II as a barracks for soldiers. It became a National Historic Site in 1970.

Fort Point, with its three tiers of casemates and an 1864 lighthouse, is dwarfed by the Golden Gate Bridge above.

## WALKING AROUND FORT POINT

You will walk into Fort Point through its sally port, a highly fortified arch that is the only point of entry. You will find a map, brochures, informative signs, and a gift shop that offers books, video materials, and other items pertaining to the fort specifically and the San Francisco Bay Area in general.

On the main floor's open area stands the Garrison Gin, which originally stood on the barbette level. The gin, short for "engine," is a block-and-tackle apparatus that raised cannons to the top tier from the ground floor. It could lift up to 17,000 pounds, while the heaviest cannon was 15,000 pounds.

The lighthouse atop the fort was in service from 1863 until 1934, the third lighthouse to stand at Fort Point.

Primary attractions are on the second floor—the Officers' Quarters—which features furnished rooms and many interesting exhibits. But please take special care on the winding staircases: they are narrow, steep, and have no hand railings. There are also less harrowing metal staircases. I do recommend going all the way up to the barbette tier, as you will get a spectacular view of the bay, the Golden Gate Bridge, and San Francisco's wonderful skyline.

### WHEN YOU GO

*From Fisherman's Wharf, find your way to U.S. Highway 101, which for much of urban San Francisco means Van Ness Avenue going south to north and Lombard Street going west toward the Golden Gate Bridge. Bay Street is a good choice to head west from the wharf, since it goes straight to Van Ness. Turn left on Van Ness and then take a right at the next light, which is Lombard (and U.S. Highway 101). Follow Highway 101 until the last exit before the Golden Gate Bridge, which will have a sign for Fort Point. (There is a backstreet way to get from the wharf to Fort Point, but the route I have provided seemed simpler to explain. If you have a GPS device, it will likely take you on that backstreet route.)*

***Important Note:*** *At this writing, Fort Point National Historic Site is open only three days a week: Friday, Saturday, and Sunday.*

# CHINA CAMP

China Camp, a small fishing village that is now part of a beautiful state park on the shores of San Pablo Bay, tells an important story about the Chinese in the San Francisco area.

In 1879, John McNear leased twelve acres of land on the shores of the bay to Richard Bullis, who in turn sublet the land to Chinese shrimp fishermen. The settlement that became known as China Camp was one of five fishing villages that grew around Point San Pedro, north of San Rafael. Because maritime regulations decreed that only white men could be captains of ships forty feet or longer, Bullis made weekly voyages to circumvent the law for his Chinese lessees, who eventually made up a camp of 469 people, all adult males except 50 and all from Kwantung Province in China.

The camp featured a school, a barbershop, three mercantiles, and a marine supply store.

Within five years, the shrimping operation was extremely successful, with the fishermen using efficient bag nets that utilized the actions of the tides. Between 1885 and 1892, the average annual catch for the entire bay was 5.4 million pounds of shrimp, virtually all of it dried and exported to China. China Camp was one of the leading producers of bay shrimp.

Shrimping became an important California industry, but the Chinese fishermen were attacked on two fronts: by white fishermen who resented their hardworking rivals and by conservationists who feared that the bay was being severely overfished.

In 1901, the California legislature passed a law banning fishing during the height of the season and in 1905 passed another prohibiting the exportation of dried shrimp, effectively crippling the industry.

In the following year, two disasters hit the Chinese living in Northern California. The first was a suspicious fire that destroyed Pacific Grove's Chinese section, and the second was the great earthquake and fire that destroyed San Francisco. As a result, many Chinese found refuge in a tent city at China Camp, a place largely out of business but, because of its isolation, free from persecution. By 1911, laws were passed prohibiting the use of bag nets and making the possession of dried shrimp unlawful. The industry was moribund for four years and would never fully recover.

The pier extending from China Camp is usually closed to the public, but I was able to get this shot because a lone fisherman was tending his boat and the gate was open.

From this pier in San Pablo Bay the China Camp fishermen launched the most successful shrimping operation in Northern California—so successful that the California legislature passed laws restricting their trade.

In 1915, some restrictions were eased, and China Camp came back to limited life into the 1930s. Eventually only one company remained, operated by the Quan family, who were the last Chinese fishermen on San Pablo Bay. The remains of their company stand at China Camp today.

## WALKING AROUND CHINA CAMP

Those remains consist of almost a dozen buildings under roof. A visitors center located in a shrimp-drying shed displays memorabilia and photographs. Nearby stands a long brick heater covered by a wooden roof where shrimp were dried using blowing fans (although the process was less efficient than simply sun-drying the catch). The remainder of China Camp consists of a pier, residences, a

The shrimp-drying shed at China Camp contains items common to the town's fishermen. The signs read, left to right, "Safety on Land and Sea," "Get What You Wish," and "Peace and Prosperity."

Flying A gasoline pump (featuring fuel at 49.9¢ per gallon), and a small cafe. The cafe formerly offered Tacoma beer ("Best From East to West"), cooked crab, and shrimp cocktail. You can still purchase the latter when it is open on weekends.

## WHEN YOU GO

*From Fort Point, return to U.S. Highway 101 and proceed north, across the Golden Gate Bridge, for 14.4 miles to the North San Pedro Road exit, which has a sign marked for China Camp State Park. Go east on North San Pedro Road for 4.7 miles. There you will find the park office, which has a helpful brochure and map. The village is 0.4 of a mile beyond the park office.*

***Important Note:*** *This state park is the fifth and final park in this book that was slated to close in 2012 due to budgetary shortfalls. If the park is barricaded so that you cannot see the fishing village of China Camp itself (there are also campgrounds and hiking trails in the camp), then ghost town seekers probably should not go at all. I definitely recommend going to the website given on page 13 to determine the status of this state park.*

# LOCKE

Locke is a town with an unusual history and considerable architectural charm. It came into being in 1916 when a group of Chinese leased land from the brothers George, Clay, and Lloyd Locke to construct residences and businesses after nearby Walnut Grove's Chinatown had burned the previous year. The Chinese could only lease land because California's Alien Land Act, passed in 1913, prohibited Asians from owning land. (Incredibly, that law was not repealed until deemed unconstitutional in 1952.)

The community known as Locke (pronounced by non-English-speaking Chinese as "Lockee") was built in less than a year using Chinese capital but white carpenters. With a resident population of about 600 and about 1,000 more during various crop-growing seasons, Locke contained every imaginable legitimate business—grocery stores, shoe repair shops, slaughterhouses, canneries, and gambling halls. The gambling halls were considered quite respectable, as they also served as social halls and a place to secure laborers. But there were many illegitimate enterprises as well: opium dens, brothels (run and staffed by whites), and speakeasies during Prohibition flourished in hidden back rooms and second stories of otherwise legal enterprises. Locke had no official law enforcement.

The citizens of Locke were primarily agricultural workers who traveled among neighboring farms harvesting a variety of crops, with asparagus and Bartlett pears prominent among them.

Most of the town's remaining Chinese residents have lived long lives in Locke, but the younger generation has largely left for more lucrative opportunities elsewhere. Locke was placed on the National Register of Historic Places in 1971 and remains the last rural Chinese town in the United States.

## WALKING AROUND LOCKE

When you arrive in Locke from the south, you will see a row of wooden buildings on the east side of River Road across from a large warehouse. These are unusual because, as they face west, they are actually the second stories of structures whose first stories face east on Main Street, the next street over. For example, the seventh building from the south once served as a theater for traveling Chinese repertory companies. Its first floor, facing east on Main, was a gambling hall.

Go north to Locke Street, turn right, and park in the nearby lot. Then take a stroll along a street unique in the West, featuring fragile wood structures with overhanging second-story balconies.

The first building of note, the Joe Shoong School, is on the northwest corner of Locke and Main. The 1926 school was funded by and named for the millionaire founder of the National Dollar stores. Students did not attend this school for their regular studies; they would attend classes after returning home from a segregated Asian elementary school in Walnut Grove. At the Joe Shoong School they learned about Chinese art, culture, and language.

The west side of Main Street in Locke features buildings whose second stories face River Road, one street west.

Kee Sing's former grocery store, the Dai Loy Gambling Hall (now a museum), and Al's Place, a popular restaurant and bar, stand on Locke's Main Street.

The other buildings on the west side of the street are the ones whose second stories you saw one block west.

The business that is likely to be the center of activity when you visit, especially if it is a weekend, stands in the middle of Main Street's east side. It is Al's Place, built in 1916 as Lee Bing's Restaurant. It was purchased by Al Adami in 1941 and has been known by the wonderfully politically incorrect name of "Al the Wop's" ever since. Have you ever slathered peanut butter on a steak? It is *de rigueur* at Al's (and delicious).

The former Locke China Imports faces River Road, while its first floor serves as a commercial building on Main Street.

Locke's most fascinating building is the Dai Loy ("Big Welcome") Gambling Hall, home of Locke's museum. In addition to historical photos, the museum features gaming tables, lottery baskets, and other gambling paraphernalia. The Dai Loy has a wonderful, dark, even mysterious mood about it.

The museum sells a booklet, "Discovering Locke," which has a helpful map for exploring the town, along with a brief history of the community. For more information, consider purchasing *Bitter Melon*, which contains interviews with Locke residents. From that volume comes a simple, telling reason to explore this picturesque town: "Locke is the most visible monument to the extraordinary efforts made by the Chinese to develop agriculture in California and establish communities in rural America."

## WHEN YOU GO

*Locke is about 82 miles east-northeast of China Camp. From China Camp, return to U.S. Highway 101 and proceed south to San Rafael. Take Interstate 580 southeast over the Richmond Bridge for 8.7 miles to Richmond. Take the Cutting Boulevard/Harbour Way exit and drive 2.4 miles east on Cutting Boulevard to the Interstate 80 onramp. Take Interstate 80 going northeast toward Sacramento for 8 miles until you see California Highway 4 exiting toward Hercules and Stockton. Take Highway 4 for 29 miles through Concord, Pittsburg, and Antioch until California Highway 160 branches off to the northeast. Stay on Highway 160 for 16.9 miles to Isleton. Shortly beyond Isleton, Highway 160 crosses the Sacramento River, but you can stay on the southeast bank, which is Isleton Road, to Walnut Grove, 9.3 miles beyond Isleton. (Both Highway 160 and Isleton Road go to Walnut Grove.) Locke is 0.6 of a mile north of Walnut Grove. Incidentally, both Isleton and Walnut Grove are interesting communities worthy of your inspection.*

## Black Diamond Mines

On your way between China Camp and Locke, the final entry in this chapter, stands a regional preserve that reminds us that not all mining was for precious metals.

Somersville and its four vanished neighbors—Nortonville, Stewartville, West Hartley, and Judsonville—made up the Mount Diablo Coal Field, which produced almost four million tons of coal between 1860 and 1914 in the state's largest coal-mining district. Although not as precious as gold, silver, or copper, coal nevertheless can be a "black diamond" when found in substantial quantities.

The town was named for Francis Somers, who in 1859 was one of the discoverers of the Black Diamond vein. The town grew to a population of about 1,000 and featured wooden homes and businesses on practically treeless, grassy, rolling hills. That is a natural combination for fire, and the business district of Nortonville, Somersville's larger neighbor to the west, was destroyed in 1878.

A total of nearly four million tons of coal were extracted from what became California's largest coal-mining operation. But in 1885, the Black Diamond Company ceased operations when superior coal deposits were found in Washington. The company took some fortunate Mount Diablo miners with them. Of the ones left behind, the Contra Costa *Gazette* declared sadly, "The few inhabitants still remaining are hopelessly stranded, with no possibility of relief."

Although some coal mining continued until the beginning of World War I, the best days were over. Dozens of buildings from Somersville and its sister coal towns were dismantled for salvage or moved to nearby communities and ranches. The last mining in the area, from the 1920s until 1949, was for a commodity even less precious than coal—silica-laden sand for a glass company in Oakland and a steel foundry in nearby Pittsburg.

The coal towns are gone, but the Black Diamond Mines Regional Preserve, a hiking and picnicking area, remains to protect the remnants of Mt. Diablo's mining history.

At the park's entrance stands the Sidney Flats Visitor Center. On your left stand several buildings, some of which formerly stood at Somersville. The town itself was located near the park's parking lot, almost a mile south.

The second visitors center is located a quarter of a mile beyond the parking area in the Greathouse Portal, one of the tunnels of the Hazel Atlas sand mining operation. At this writing, it is temporarily closed to widen the entrance and improve structural stability in the tunnel. When it reopens, memorabilia, photographs, and a video will provide a closer look at the now-vanished coal communities. You can also take an hour-and-a-half-long tour of the Hazel Atlas Mine, but tours are limited to fifteen people on a first-come, first-served basis.

On a hill west of the Somersville site is the Rose Hill Cemetery, the best—but bittersweet—ghost town reason to visit the Black Diamond preserve. The cemetery, which is a ten- to fifteen-minute hike from the picnic area, has many interesting and touching headstones and an excellent overview of the Somersville site. Many nationalities are represented in the cemetery with a preponderance of Welsh. As you might expect, several buried here died in mine accidents.

Those who explore old cemeteries are accustomed to seeing a large number of children's graves, but this graveyard has a disturbing percentage of headstones for the young, many of whom died of diphtheria, typhoid, and scarlet fever. Four children of the Jenkins family, for example, died within seven years of each other, none reaching the age of nine. Three children of David and Lizzie Bowman are buried here; none lived to the age of two. The epitaph of Julia Etta, who died in 1870 at two years of age, could apply for all the children: "Too sweet a flower to bloom on earth, she has gone to bloom in heaven."

The Black Diamond Mines Regional Preserve is southeast of Pittsburg and southwest of Antioch on your route between China Camp and Locke. On California Highway 4 between Pittsburg and Antioch, take the Somersville Road South exit. Take Somersville Road south for 2.8 miles, following signs to the regional preserve.

The Rose Hill Cemetery lies almost equidistant between the sites of Nortonville and Somersville. Looking east beyond the cemetery is the site of Somersville.

# 5

# GHOSTS
## O F   T H E
# EASTERN
# SIERRA

THIS CHAPTER FEATURES TWO OF THE VERY BEST GHOST TOWNS IN THE AMERICAN WEST: Bodie and Cerro Gordo. It also displays some of the West's most spectacular scenery, because you'll be looking at some of the highest peaks in the contiguous states of our nation, including the highest, Mt. Whitney, at an elevation of 14,505 feet. Furthermore, you are likely to find something fairly rare in California—relative solitude, because you will be in Mono and Inyo Counties, the fourth- and sixth- least populated of the fifty-eight counties in California. The eastern slopes of the Sierra Nevada are far more rugged than its western slopes (where the Gold Rush began), and the high desert below the mountains has a desolate beauty. Combine that with the eerie splendor of Mono Lake and the proximity of Yosemite National Park and you have a superb backcountry destination.

One important caveat: the weather in both Mono and Inyo Counties can quickly go from glorious to severe. Summer affords the best opportunity to see the first ghost town, incomparable Bodie, because it is located at an elevation of 8,375 feet and has ten to twenty feet of snow in the winter. The remaining sites are in the Owens Valley and can likely be visited year-round.

When you explore this chapter, in addition to Bodie and Cerro Gordo, you will see two sets of wonderful charcoal kilns, a railroad ghost town, and a site that is one of the most melancholy places in the West.

A reconstruction of one of the eight guard towers that stood at Manzanar.

On the headstone:
EVELYN,
BELOVED
DAUGHTER OF
FANNIE O.
& ALBERT K.
MYERS,
BORN MAY 1, 1894,
DIED APRIL 5, 1897.

A beautiful headstone for the beloved Evelyn, at Bodie.

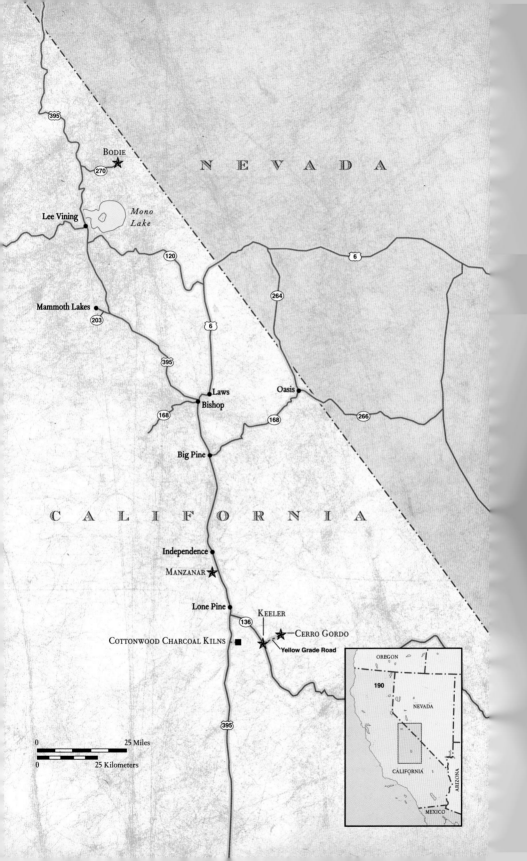

# BODIE

Bodie is one of a kind. No ghost town has as much remaining from its heyday, and no place is maintained like Bodie. Now a state park, it is kept in a state of "arrested decay," which means that it is not being restored to its original condition but rather preserved in its present shape. When shingles or windows need replacement, they are identical to the original. Many buildings that have a charming lean are actually braced from within by specially trained carpenters.

And what buildings they are! Almost 170 remain, most of them made of wind-battered and sun-bleached wood. Although the majority are residences, Bodie also has a variety of commercial and mining-related structures. As many buildings as there are, they represent only one in twenty of Bodie's total number, as fires in 1892 and 1932 ravaged the town.

Although Bodie is a state park, it does not feel like one; there are no tourist concession stands, no multimedia presentations, and no modern automobiles. There are also no food stands, so bring your own fare to eat. And you will need sustenance, because you will want to spend at least three hours in Bodie. In fact, if you hope to see most of it, I recommend staying all day (or spend parts of two days: see Insider's Tips at the end of this entry). I have visited more than six hundred ghost towns in twelve states, and this one is the best.

Buildings at Bodie often lean at precipitous angles, but many are propped or braced to keep them standing.

The 1879 Bon Ton Lodging House became Bodie's schoolhouse after a delinquent burned down its predecessor.

Only four years after the discovery of gold, the Mother Lode was saturated with Argonauts. Late entrants found little opportunity for success and so ventured elsewhere. One of those disappointed prospectors was Waterman (or William— accounts differ) S. Body (also spelled "Bodey"), who came from Sonora to the Eastern Sierra after gold was discovered in Mono County in 1857. In 1859, Body and a partner, E. S. "Black" Taylor, headed into the hills and found gold in Taylor Gulch, named for the partner, where they built a cabin.

Body, from Poughkeepsie, New York, never saw the glory of their discovery, as he died the next year in a snowstorm while bringing supplies to the cabin.

A mining district was formed including Taylor Gulch on July 10, 1860. The first recorded spelling of the camp as "Bodie" appeared in October 1862. Emil Billeb, a Bodie resident for decades, says the name was spelled that way because of a careless sign painter, but others claim it was a deliberate change because, spelled "Body," people were pronouncing it "bah-dee," not "*boh*-dee."

During the 1860s, Bodie enjoyed only modest prosperity, partly because of gold strikes across the Nevada border at Aurora, which boomed from 1861 until 1869. But Bodie's turn came when out-of-work Aurora and Virginia City miners reexamined Bodie Bluff.

The only way to visit Bodie's Standard Mine and Mill complex is to take an informative tour.

The bonanza began in 1874, and two years later a cave-in at the Bunker Hill Mine exposed a rich concentration of gold ore. In 1878, a huge strike at the Bodie Mine brought a million dollars' worth of ore in only six weeks. In that year, Bodie's population reached about 3,000 people. Two years later, the population had more than tripled.

Building a metropolis at an elevation of more than 8,000 feet was no simple matter. The Bodie area is virtually treeless. Lumber for buildings and wood for fuel were freighted from a forest thirty-two miles away, south of Mono Lake, creating a lumber boomtown there called Mono Mills. In 1881 a narrow-gauge railroad from Mono Mills to Bodie made wood shipments cheaper and more reliable. It was a good thing, too, because Bodie's mines and mills consumed 45,000 cords of wood annually. (To visit the almost vanished site of Mono Mills, take U.S. Highway 395 south from Lee Vining for 5 miles to California Highway 120. Turn east and proceed 9.1 miles. An historic plaque, one concrete foundation, pinkish stone blocks, and scattered timber remain.)

Mono Mills' lumber created a boisterous Bodie, with sixty-five saloons and gambling halls, seven breweries, and a red-light district on Bonanza Street, which was facetiously known as Maiden Lane or Virgin Alley. The jail was conveniently located immediately east of Bonanza. A minister in 1881 proclaimed the place "a sea of sin, lashed by the tempests of lust and passion."

A "sea of sin" is naturally going to have its share of violence as well. Bodie became notorious for its shootings and murders, and citizens were so accustomed to the mayhem that a corpse discovered in the morning was known as "a man for breakfast."

But that is only one version of Bodie. Popular histories tend to emphasize, even glorify, the violent and tempestuous nature of bonanza camps, as if drunken, bawdy, and murderous behavior was both accepted and the norm. It was neither. Grant H. Smith, later a respected mining attorney, came to Bodie at age fourteen in 1879 and served as a telegraph messenger boy. As a result, he entered every imaginable social and business situation. He counters Bodie's scurrilous reputation, saying, "These men, as a rule, were virile, enthusiastic, and free-living, bound by

The door is open at the 1882 Methodist Church in Bodie, one of only a few buildings you can actually enter.

The Dechambeau Hotel, the I.O.O.F. Hall (with the Bodie Athletic Club downstairs), the Miners Union Hall, and the town morgue stand left to right along Bodie's Main Street.

very few of the rules of conventional society. However, they had an admirable code of ethics: liberal-minded, generous to a fault, square-dealing, and completely devoid of pretense and hypocrisy. . . . A friend in Bodie was a friend for life."

But Bodie's reputation, Smith's efforts notwithstanding, will forever be tainted toward its lawless side by one famous quote, uttered by a little girl whose family was moving from Aurora to the infamous town. In her evening prayer, she was overheard by her parents saying, "Goodbye, God, I'm going to Bodie." Aurora journalists used the prayer to ridicule Bodie, but Bodie journalists, in a rejoinder, insisted that the tone and punctuation were vastly different. What the little girl had actually said was "Good! By God, I'm going to Bodie!"

Bodie's boom times lasted a mere three years. During its peak, almost fifty mines were producing ore that was fed to ten mills with a combined 162 stamps. By 1882, however, the population had dropped drastically from about 10,000 to less than 500. In 1883, Bodie mine stocks crashed. The town was virtually lifeless.

During the bonanza years, an estimated $21 million in gold had been extracted. Naturally, some refused to believe that Bodie's glory days were over, and one of those became the person crucial to Bodie's present-day state of preservation—James Stuart Cain.

Jim Cain came from Canada in 1875 at age twenty-one looking to find his fortune in Carson City, Nevada, just when the Comstock Lode was in decline. Like many others, he went to Bodie, arriving in 1879.

Cain began in the lumber and freighting business. As Bodie boomed, he supplied much of the wood, transporting it across Mono Lake by barge. As he prospered, he diversified by investing in mines and leasing the Bodie Railroad and Lumber Company, which replaced his barge. When Bodie plummeted, Cain stayed, buying bargain-rate mines and the Bodie Bank.

In 1890, Cain brought to Bodie the then-new cyanide process to treat previously worthless tailings. To lower costs at the highly successful cyanide plants, he brought electric power to Bodie, the first use of electricity generated over long-distance lines (the hydroelectric plant was thirteen miles away). The technology was so untested that power lines were laid in a straight line, for fear that if the line curved, the electricity might jump off into space.

The successful use of long-distance electricity at Bodie caused a revolution in the way mines were powered and changed the way the world produced ore.

The cyanide tailings process kept Bodie profitable into the early twentieth century, but Cain was convinced that Bodie would have another windfall from new gold deposits.

One constant in all these dealings was Cain's Bodie Bank. Although he was a banker, Cain hardly fit the stereotype. His bank, for example, had calendars featuring pin-up girls on its walls.

Moreover, Cain was known for his practical jokes. His bank had one of Bodie's earliest telephones, and a Chinese businessman (after being convinced that the phone could "speak" Chinese as well as English) often used it to call the Wells Fargo agent in Hawthorne, Nevada, for an update on his produce order. He invariably inquired about sweet potatoes, so, on one occasion, Cain called the agent in advance to alert him and then placed three sweet potatoes in the phone's battery box. When the gentleman inquired about sweet potatoes, the agent informed him he would send them immediately by wire. Cain then ceremoniously opened the battery box, and the sweet potatoes dropped to the floor. The stupefied grocer requested that the entire order be sent by wire.

The billiard table inside the Wheaton and Hollis Hotel in Bodie, with elegant lions supporting it, leans to give a house player a true advantage. The photo was taken through the glass of the front window.

Another photo taken through glass shows the interior of Bodie's Boone Store and Warehouse. Notice the shelves that feature merchandise ready for "sale."

Cain operated the bank for forty years, until 1932. He would open every weekday at 10 a.m. to no customers. In that year, a boy playing with matches started a fire that leveled about two-thirds of Bodie's largely vacant business district. The fire consumed Cain's bank, although the vault held and the safe inside protected its contents. In that same year, Cain left Bodie for good, moving to San Francisco where he died in 1939 at age eighty-five.

But Cain's legacy did not die. He had the foresight to hire a watchman to protect the town, and in 1962 Bodie became a state park. Because of Jim Cain, Bodie stands as a monument to the rush for riches in the American West.

## WALKING AROUND BODIE

An outstanding brochure you can purchase when you enter Bodie suggests a logical walking tour. Remember to peer into every building through as many windows as you can to study its contents.

For example, if you gaze into the living room window of the Metzger House on Fuller Street, you will see a dusty old doll carriage, a wooden sled, and a small toy dog for a child to sit on and rock, like a hobby horse.

James B. Perry's stone is one of the most artistic I have seen. From quarried stone evolves a kind of parchment announcing that he was a native of Ireland and served as a Supervisor of Mono County. Note that the "parchment" even is rolled at the bottom and has a turned "edge" at the upper right.

In Sam Leon's Bar on Main Street, you squint into the semidarkness to make out roulette tables, a bar, a one-armed bandit, and gaming tables stacked with chips as if waiting for the next hand.

A comment I have heard several times on my visits to Bodie is that it is unfortunate that we can only gaze through the windows of most buildings. But if we could step inside, floors would have to be reinforced, valuable objects would have to be placed out of reach, and the whole feeling of Bodie—that people up and left in a moment—would be seriously compromised. The town is much more genuine because we cannot enter most structures.

In the center of town, on Main Street south of Green Street, stands the 1878 Miners Union Hall, which houses the park's interesting museum. While in the hall, consider purchasing tickets to one of the park's outstanding tours.

The most frequently offered tour is of the huge 1899 Standard Mill, east of town on the slopes of Bodie Bluff. Tours are given as if you were a 1905 prospective employee, a delightful illusion that makes the experience more genuine.

Two other tours go into otherwise closed-off areas, including the train depot and mine shafts. They do not run daily, however, and are given but once a day when offered, so inquire before you visit.

The 1879 Bodie Schoolhouse, on Green east of Main, offers one of the most fascinating glances into Bodie's past. Originally the Bon Ton Lodging House, the building was pressed into educational service when a delinquent burned down the first school. When you peer through the windows, notice textbooks on desks and a wooden globe whose maps have peeled off, leaving it merely a large wooden ball. A wall clock, appropriately, has no hands.

Bodie's cemetery (actually three adjoining graveyards) is 0.3 of a mile southwest of town. The site is well worth exploring, and not just because of its many interesting headstones. It also features an overview of Bodie, making it a natural stop for photographers. An informative cemetery guide is usually available at the gate for purchase or loan.

Two of the most beautifully carved headstones I have ever seen stand in the Bodie cemetery. One, for James B. Perry, looks like quarried rock, but from it flows a graceful, curving parchment from which we learn that Perry died in 1896 at sixty-three years of age and served as a Mono County supervisor. A similar marker, certainly crafted by the same stonemason, stands nearby for Danish native Annie C. Fouke.

One story that the cemetery guide does not tell is about the now-missing Pagdin family headstone. It was made of hollow iron, with detachable bolts holding the front and rear plates. During Prohibition, a customer would remove the bolts and leave money. A bootlegger would slide to the cemetery and leave a cache of liquor. As longtime resident Emil Billeb put it, "After Repeal there were noticeably fewer mourners visiting the cemetery."

After you have completed your tour of Bodie, you might recall those journalists who doctored the little Aurora girl's prayer. In a way, they were speaking for present-day ghost town enthusiasts—Bodie has become our mecca, and now we can justifiably say, "Good! By God, I'm going to Bodie!"

*Insider's Tips: Here are two suggestions from someone who has visited Bodie many times. One: If you are a photographer, enter Bodie in the afternoon and remain until it closes, stay overnight nearby, and return first thing the next morning. Be at the entrance booth before the park opens. I was there on a morning in August, one of the town's busiest months, and I was the only tourist in the park for almost an hour. You can get a lot done in that time. When I was leaving, there was a steady stream of cars heading toward Bodie. Two: The two closest places to stay with multiple services are Bridgeport and Lee Vining. But my favorite is only ten minutes south of Lee Vining at the town of June Lake. It is in an almost Bavarian setting, rooms are a better value for the dollar, and several restaurants are quite good.*

## WHEN YOU GO

*From Lee Vining, drive 18.3 miles north on U.S. Highway 395. Turn east on California Highway 270 and proceed 12.3 miles to the state park. All but the last 2.7 miles are paved. In good weather, even motor homes traverse the route.*

**Note:** *Bodie is less than 125 miles from Nevada's Virginia City, the heart of the famous Comstock Lode and a tourist destination with dozens of wonderful buildings. It is, in many ways, the ghost town antithesis of Bodie, but it is delightful in its own way. For information on Virginia City, consult my book* Ghost Towns of the Mountain West *(also from Voyageur Press).*

# MANZANAR

Present-day visitors to the Owens Valley cannot imagine how it looked in the early 1900s. Once the center of a promising fruit-growing industry, the area now has a distinctly parched look to it.

Manzanar, "apple orchard" in Spanish, began as an agricultural community in 1910. Several thousand acres were cultivated for apples, peaches, pears, alfalfa, and potatoes. The new town received a post office in 1911. Since 1905, however, the Los Angeles Department of Water and Power had been quietly acquiring water rights in the Owens Valley with the purpose of diverting Owens Valley water to the flourishing "City of Angels." When the Los Angeles Aqueduct was completed in 1913, the land acquisition increased, and by 1929 Los Angeles owned all of the land encompassing Manzanar. The town was abandoned by the 1930s. For diehard Owens Valley residents, the loss of their water was a cruel blow. Many current residents still speak with great bitterness over the "theft" of their water. As respected Inyo County historian W. A. Chalfant once wrote, "The government held Owens Valley while Los Angeles skinned it." Or, as Will Rogers put it, "This was a wonderful valley with a quarter million acres of fruit and alfalfa. But Los Angeles had to have more water for its chamber of commerce to drink more toasts to its growth, more water to dilute its orange juice. . . . So, now this is the valley of desolation."

A Japanese-style entrance station stands at Manzanar, with the auditorium in the right background.

Manzanar's cemetery contains an obelisk memorializing those who died at Manzanar. Most of the remains were moved elsewhere.

In 1942, Manzanar, by then merely a place name in the desert, became a community of more than 10,000 people in one of this country's sorriest episodes. On February 19th, 1942, seventy-four days after the attack on Honolulu's Pearl Harbor, Executive Order 9066 commanded all persons of Japanese ancestry who lived on the West Coast of California, Oregon, and Washington to report, beginning on March 30th of that year, for transportation to "relocation centers" in areas that the government deemed to be nonstrategic during wartime. In all, 120,313 people, most of them American citizens, lived for a maximum of three-and-a-half years in ten relocation centers in remote areas of California, Arizona, Colorado, Idaho, Wyoming, Utah, and Arkansas. (Incidentally, Canada conducted a similar program. For more information, consult my book *Ghost Towns of the Pacific Northwest*, forthcoming from Voyageur Press.)

The first center to be completed was Manzanar, through which 11,070 internees were eventually processed, about two-thirds of whom were American citizens. The rest were aliens; however, most of them had lived in the United States for decades but were denied citizenship by discriminatory laws.

The peak population of Manzanar reached 10,046 in September 1942, but it dwindled to about 6,000 by 1944 as it became more and more clear to authorities that the Japanese Americans posed no war threat. The last of the internees were allowed to leave in November 1945, three months after the war had ended. Manzanar was dismantled, with many of the buildings sold and moved to nearby communities.

## WALKING AND DRIVING AROUND MANZANAR

If you value fundamental human rights and the right to due process, you need to visit Manzanar.

When I first saw Manzanar in 1982, it was a true ghost town, with a California Historical Landmark plaque and two sentry posts, then filled with graffiti, much of it written in Japanese and several signed by people who identified themselves as former internees. There appeared to be little else to indicate the enormous size of the place until I drove down street after street, some faded into mere ruts, others clearly visible. Occasional foundations and scattered rusted debris began to appear before me as my eyes started to learn to look more carefully. Dead trees stood in rows in what was obviously once an orchard. In a few places I discovered rock gardens and empty ponds that clearly were attempts, in this bleak place, to add touches of beauty.

On the western edge of the property was a small cemetery with a white memorial obelisk. I photographed it and took a print to two separate Japanese American students at the University of Arizona for translation. One read it as "the monument of comforting the soul," while the other told me it said "the monument for the consolation of the spirits." Each said the obelisk, to them, was an image of great sadness. They understood completely when I explained to them where it was and why it was there.

As I was leaving Manzanar on that first visit, I noticed a large Inyo County maintenance facility that I surmised was from the era of the relocation center. I drove in and learned from the employees that the building was Manzanar's gymnasium and auditorium, complete with stage and projection booth. I wandered through the facility, fascinated.

Today that maintenance building has been completely restored and turned into the interpretive center of the Manzanar National Historic Site, and much has changed at the former relocation center since my first visit—all for the better.

I made no attempt, in the historical section of this entry, to convey what the internees must have experienced at Manzanar or the other relocation centers. I have

A 1940s Ford stake bed truck stands in front of a reconstruction of one of Manzanar's mess halls.

visited three others in the United States: Heart Mountain, Wyoming; Minidoka, Idaho; and Topaz, Utah. (I have also visited four in British Columbia.) In each location I felt an emptiness, a bleakness that permeated the sites. But I couldn't imagine what it was like to be forced to live there. If you want to learn about the life at these places, commit yourself to spending plenty of time at the Manzanar interpretive center. The excellent and very touching displays, films, maps, models, reconstructions, and recordings will give you at least some insight into what the internees endured. The center also has an extensive collection of books for sale on the war internment. But you will also see photos of high school bands, sports teams, and social activities as the Japanese Americans attempted to make the best of their situation.

When you complete your investigation in the interpretive center, be sure to walk outside and see the buildings that have been reconstructed on the site. At this writing, there are two barracks, a mess hall, and Guard Tower #8. I was told that additional structures likely will be added.

Then return to your car to take the driving tour of the grounds using an available brochure. Whereas I wandered rather aimlessly around the grounds on my first visit, you will have the advantage of a guided tour.

After you have finished your experience at Manzanar, you might want to re-read the historical plaque near the sentry post. It concludes with this thought: "May the injustices and humiliation suffered here as a result of hysteria, racism, and economic exploitation never emerge again."

## WHEN YOU GO

*Manzanar is 5.9 miles south of Independence and 9.9 miles north of Lone Pine on U.S. Highway 395. Independence is 106 miles south of Lee Vining, the town south of Bodie, the preceding entry in this chapter.*

## The Laws Railroad Museum and Historic Site

In between Bodie and Manzanar stands a wonderful railroad museum and historic town.

Laws was a stop along the Carson & Colorado Railroad, which extended from Mound House, Nevada, to Keeler, California. (For more on that railroad, see the Keeler entry, page 173.) The rails reached Laws in 1883, but some keen foresight had ensured that when the tracks made it to Laws, a water tank, a turntable, a depot, an agent's house, and a section boss's house had already been erected.

As you might expect, all this activity brought people and businesses to Laws, such as a boarding house, an eating house, a pool hall and dance hall, two general stores, and a post office. Nearby farms and ranches were developed to take advantage of the cheap shipping of commodities that the railroad afforded.

The railroad ceased operating in 1959, leading, naturally, to the decline of the small community. In fact, Laws all but disappeared for salvage except for the depot, the agent's house, the turntable, and fuel and water tanks. Concerned citizens in nearby Bishop and the Owens Valley combined to save a series of buildings and move them to Laws, which had been donated to Bishop and Inyo County by the Southern Pacific Railroad in 1964, resulting in the charming historic town that exists there today.

Laws includes far more than railroad memorabilia, featuring a general store, a post office, a print shop, a fire station, the 1909 North Inyo Schoolhouse, and much more. But the depot and Engine #9, its freight cars, and an 1883 Carson & Colorado caboose dominate the scene. Another attraction anyone interested in ghost towns must see is the completely restored and operating 1927 self-propelled Brill railcar that once ferried passengers along the Death Valley Railroad. For more on that line, see the Ryan entry, page 190.

Laws is located 4.5 miles northeast of Bishop on U.S. Highway 6.

**Note:** *A second excellent place to explore is the Eastern California Museum, which features displays of settlers, Indians, and soldiers; historical photos of the area; and an outdoor display including buildings, wagons, and implements that were brought to the museum to give a representation of life in the early days of the pioneers of the Eastern Sierra and Owens Valley. It is located in Independence, almost 6 miles north of a previous entry, Manzanar.*

Engine #9, a narrow-gauge 4-6-0 locomotive, looks ready to haul the freight of the Carson & Colorado Railroad at the Laws Railroad Museum. In the foreground is the 1883 Laws depot. *Photograph by Michael Moore*

# THE COTTONWOOD CHARCOAL KILNS

The remarkable silver deposits at Cerro Gordo (see page 166) affected the entire Owens Valley. A shipping point at Keeler (see page173), a smelter at Swansea (west of Keeler), and these amazing charcoal kilns near the western shore of now dry Owens Lake all owe their existence to the travails involved in getting supplies into and silver out of the boomtown of Cerro Gordo.

Kilns were crucial to the mining process. The smelting of ore, which eliminates the impurities still in ore after the milling process, requires enormous heat. The materials available in the late 1800s for creating that heat were wood and coal, both of which burn too quickly and produce too little heat to be efficient. Kilns were used to convert a fast-burning, low-heat substance into a slow-burning, high-heat fuel. Wood was turned to charcoal; coal became coke. Although wood and coal cannot efficiently fire a smelter, charcoal and coke can.

These kilns and the ones at Wildrose Canyon (see page 183) converted wood to charcoal by heating wood in a controlled-burn process. Wood was loaded into a ground-level opening. First dry wood, followed by green wood, was stacked as high as possible. A higher door in the rear of the kiln, which was reached through a ramp, was used to finish filling the kiln. Kilns of this size could hold up to fifty cords of wood. The doors were closed and sealed, the wood set afire, and the air within each kiln carefully regulated through vents being alternately opened and sealed.

This slow "cooking" process would take about ten days. At that time, the kilns were opened and the fire was doused with water. The charcoal was removed and, after cooling, shipped to a smelter.

The process was very similar when coal was converted to coke. For some reason, such kilns, when using coal, are called "coke ovens," not "coke kilns."

In 1873, Col. Sherman Stevens erected a sawmill on Cottonwood Creek, adjacent to large stands of trees in Cottonwood Canyon. He also constructed a flume to carry the lumber from that sawmill, along with uncut wood, to a point along the supply route to Cerro Gordo.

The wood was put into the Cottonwood Kilns and made into charcoal, which was subsequently shipped, along with the lumber from the Cottonwood Canyon sawmill, by steamer across Owens Lake and then by mule teams up to Cerro Gordo. The charcoal fueled the smelters at the mine, and the lumber was used both to construct buildings and to timber the mine.

The Cottonwood Charcoal Kilns provided fuel for the smelters at Cerro Gordo in the 1870s.

## WALKING AROUND THE COTTONWOOD CHARCOAL KILNS

Most kilns were constructed using rough stone, cut stone, or bricks. These are the only kilns I have ever seen (and I've seen hundreds scattered through Arizona, New Mexico, Colorado, Wyoming, Idaho, Montana, Washington, and California) that were made of fragile clay bricks covered in plaster. Rather than being an important relic of a major mining operation, these kilns resemble something that an ambitious sand sculptor on the beach at Santa Monica might create. The Cottonwood kilns have been scorched by sun, sand-blown by wind, and melted by rainstorms, and the fact that they still exist at all makes them well worth visiting and photographing. But they are inexorably deteriorating, especially on their south sides, and you should be certain to visit them while there is still something left to see.

### WHEN YOU GO

*The turnoff to the Cottonwood Charcoal Kilns is 13 miles south of downtown Lone Pine (and 11.1 miles south of the Eastern Sierra Interagency Visitor Center) on U.S. Highway 395. A California Historical Landmark sign directs you to the site, which is 1 mile east of the highway on a very passable, albeit washboard, dirt road.*

# CERRO GORDO

Cerro Gordo is, like Bodie, one of the best ghost towns in the American West. Bodie (see page 46) has many more buildings, but it also has something Cerro Gordo does not—many more visitors. Cerro Gordo's structures are photogenic, the artifacts are plentiful, and the twisting, steep road to the site has only been marginally improved since the 1870s. The total experience of visiting Cerro Gordo rivals any site in any of my nine ghost town books.

The silver and lead bonanza in the mountains high above Owens Lake made Los Angeles a city. If that seems like an impossible exaggeration, consider the Los Angeles *News* in 1870: "To this city, the Owens River trade is invaluable. What Los Angeles is, is mainly due to it."

In 1865, Pablo Flores and two other Mexicans found rich silver ore deposits near Cerro Gordo Peak (*cerro gordo* means "fat hill" in Spanish, referring either to the rounded shapes of the mountains or, more likely, that they were "fat"—meaning "rich"—in ore). Because of the size and depth of the vein, a shipping route was established through the Owens Valley that gave the sleepy Pueblo de Los Angeles ("City of the Angels") the bulk of its transportation and supply business. Los Angeles didn't just grow; it exploded: hence the remark in the Los Angeles *News*.

In 1867, the Lone Pine Mining District was formed, which included Cerro Gordo. Two years later, San Francisco mining engineer Mortimer Belshaw arrived at Cerro Gordo, assessed the enormous profits to be made at the site, and took steps to make sure that much of those profits would be his. Shipping silver ore is much more expensive than shipping pure silver. That means smelting the ore at or near the site will increase profits. Smelting of silver requires lead, which is found in galena, which was in abundance at Cerro Gordo. As a result, Belshaw invested heavily in the Union Mine (for silver and lead) and eventually owned two of the three smelters near the mines. Perhaps the smartest thing he did was tactical: he constructed a toll road following the only practical access route (which is still used today), thus controlling the only way between Cerro Gordo and the logical shipping point at the base of the mountains. That meant he also controlled something even more precious than silver: the supply of water to the mines—and to the miners.

Victor Beaudry had arrived in Cerro Gordo before Belshaw and owned the principal store there. He saw that Belshaw was the ticket to riches at the site and became his partner. The two dominated the short but extremely prosperous life

The former company store at Cerro Gordo now serves as a museum.

One of the two Cerro Gordo assay offices stands to the left of a crib for Lola Travis' House of Pleasure. Behind stands the trestle for a tramway that extended all the way to Keeler.

The home of Billy Crapo, who shot the town postmaster and then fled, stands to the left of Cerro Gordo's American Hotel.

of Cerro Gordo. How prosperous? Between 1868 and 1875, approximately $13 million in silver-lead bullion was shipped from the smelters, making the Cerro Gordo mines the greatest producers of those metals in California's history. For seven years, California had its own Comstock Lode.

Getting the bullion to market was the responsibility of Remi Nadeau, whose mule-team freight wagons, about eighty in number, worked their way down the steep and treacherous Yellow Grade Road (Belshaw's toll road, so named for the area's yellow shale). From there they skirted the north shore of Owens Lake, headed across the Mojave Desert into Los Angeles, and finally unloaded their treasure at that city's port of San Pedro. The journey took about fifteen days each way.

The only problem was that there was too much silver to haul. The smelters were producing a staggering four hundred ingots, weighing about eighty-five pounds each, in every twenty-four-hour period, and Nadeau's freight teams could not keep up. At one point, 30,000 bars had accumulated on site, and miners stacked them to make cabins—no doubt the most expensive shacks ever built.

The solution was to shorten the freight route. In 1872, steamboats began carrying the precious cargo across Owens Lake to Cartago, on the southwestern shore. A second route was initiated a year later to pick up lumber and charcoal from Cottonwood Creek (see the preceding entry, page 164). With the new routes in place, in 1874 Remi Nadeau's freight wagons delivered more than $4 million worth of silver to Los Angeles.

By 1877, however, the mines began to play out. The last load of bullion was shipped the next year. In 1883, by the time a railroad reached Keeler (see the following entry, page 173), the prosperity was over and the reason for a railroad long past. The town's post office somehow hung on until 1895.

Cerro Gordo was not quite done yet. In 1911, Louis Gordon discovered enormous zinc deposits up in the mountains, and the once-great silver and lead producer became the principal source of high-quality zinc in the United States. Two aerial tramways were constructed to transport the ore, one from the Union Shaft at Cerro Gordo all the way to the Southern Pacific tracks at Keeler, a distance of more than four miles. The other tram ran just over a mile from the Morningstar Mine, south of the townsite, to a terminus on the Yellow Grade Road. Neither tramway required power, because the weight of the ore going down was heavier than any supplies loaded into the buckets heading back up.

The zinc operations lasted into the 1930s, when the town that built Los Angeles and gave California its own "Comstock" withered into obscurity.

Over the decades, the town was subjected to repeated vandalism and theft despite efforts by occasional caretakers, but Cerro Gordo seemed to have a solid, steady future when Jody Stewart purchased it in 1985. She was barely forty years of age and had funds available to use to restore the town, which had become a haphazard near-junkyard despite its remarkable, historic buildings. She was joined by Mike Patterson, three years her junior, as her general manager, helpmate, and, eventually, her husband. They made enormous progress over the next several years, clearing the property, shoring up buildings, and generally bringing the site back to life. Their enthusiasm and charm attracted many volunteer groups who came up for weekends to assist. I had first seen Cerro Gordo in 1982 before Jody took over. When I returned in 1989, I could not fathom how they could have improved the site as much as they had in such a relatively short time. On my next visit in 1998, I was yet again amazed at the restoration work that had been accomplished.

However, in 2001, only three years after my third visit, Jody Stewart, then Jody Stewart-Patterson, died at 57. Mike Patterson continued to work on Cerro Gordo until 2009, when he also died. I tell you this principally because I would be remiss if I didn't acknowledge my friends' enormous contributions to this marvelous ghost town. They saved Cerro Gordo so there is still a town for you to enjoy and explore. But their deaths may also have an effect upon your ability to visit Cerro Gordo. At this writing, the future of the town is uncertain: volunteers are attempting to protect the site and continue the work that has been sustained since the mid-1980s. I have provided a website address at the end of this entry; I hope it will still be current when you read this so that you may ascertain how to visit Cerro Gordo.

## WALKING AROUND CERRO GORDO

As you enter Cerro Gordo, the first structure will be on your left—the stone chimney of Victor Beaudry's smelter. Beyond it on the same side of the road stand what once served as a shop and/or a garage, now fashioned into a chapel, and behind it, the bunkhouse and what likely was an assay office.

To your right will be a string of classic Western buildings on a rise just above the road: an icehouse, a screened-in coolhouse for outdoor food storage, and the

The Cerro Gordo townsite spreads out before you, with the Owens Valley and the Sierra Nevada behind. *Photograph by Michael Moore*

wonderful 1871 American Hotel. Next to the hotel is the former residence of Billy Crapo, who killed Postmaster Harry Boland by shooting him from behind in 1893. Crapo bolted from town and was never captured. On the hills behind the hotel stand several miners' shacks.

Of these first several buildings, the American Hotel is the treasure. The two-story wooden structure features a bar, tables, a card room, a working kitchen, and furnished upstairs rooms.

The road you came in on forks beyond those first buildings. Directly in front of you on the right is the home of the town's original tycoon, Mortimer Belshaw, built around 1868. Behind his residence is a shack believed to have been the home of Belshaw's Chinese cook. Across the street from that shack is the beautifully restored 1909 home of Louis Gordon, the man who brought Cerro Gordo back to prosperity with his discovery of zinc.

Across the street from the Belshaw house is the tin-covered former general store, now a museum. When I first saw it, the store was so thoroughly surrounded by junk and trash that it was difficult even to approach. Now it features a spacious front deck.

The 1911 trestle of a tramway that sent zinc all the way to the railroad at Keeler stands above Cerro Gordo. *Photograph by Michael Moore*

Up the hill from the store is an odd pairing of wooden structures. One is believed to have been a crib for Lola Travis' House of Pleasure, a dance hall that stood behind the crib. This is the only crib still standing, although at least one other is believed to have existed next to it. Immediately adjacent to the crib is a second assay office, an unusual use of a building so close to a brothel.

The most dramatic structure in town is the trestle of the Union Shaft, the one that was built during the zinc operation that began a tramway that extended all the way to Keeler. I was standing on that trestle in 1982 when I had the most terrifying experience in all my years of ghost town exploring. I was peering through my telephoto lens down to the Owens Valley, when suddenly into focus came the nose of a jet fighter heading straight at me as it careened up the canyon. I could, for an instant, see the helmeted pilot in the cockpit. It screeched over the townsite and left me gasping and holding on to the shaking trestle. I have returned to Cerro Gordo three more times, but, strangely enough, I have not ventured again out onto that trestle. It is also much more rickety now, and you shouldn't go out there, either.

The Union Shaft hoist house, the Morningstar Mine and all mine tunnels are, at this writing, off limits to visitors.

## WHEN YOU GO

From downtown Lone Pine, head south on U.S. Highway 395 for 1.9 miles to the junction with California Highway 136 (the location of the informative Eastern Sierra Interagency Visitor Center). Drive 12.4 miles to the town of Keeler (see following entry). Just beyond the main part of Keeler is a dirt road that heads north into the mountains. A sign there indicates that it is the route to Cerro Gordo. The 7.6-mile drive up the Yellow Grade Road is, in places, very, very steep, as Cerro Gordo, at an elevation of 8,500 feet, is almost 5,000 feet above Keeler. It is often impassable in bad weather. I strongly recommend a high-clearance truck, preferably with four-wheel-drive.

**Important Note:** Cerro Gordo is privately owned. You can get information about exploring the town at www.cerrogordo.us. When you do visit the town, be sure to take your own water, as it still must be trucked up from the valley below. I also suggest a generous contribution if admission is not required.

# KEELER

As a railroad town, Keeler was, quite literally, the end of the line. Today, with the railroad long gone, it has a dusty, forlorn look that also gives it an end-of-the-line *feeling*.

In the 1870s, what is now called Keeler was known as Cerro Gordo Landing, the shipping point to cross Owens Lake for the silver and lead ore that was coming out in astonishing quantities from the mountains above town (see Cerro Gordo, the preceding entry).

The "end of the line" refers to the terminus at Keeler of the Carson & Colorado Railroad. The plan was for the narrow-gauge rail line, which was begun in 1880, to extend from one river to another, accounting for its name: from Mound House, Nevada, on the Carson River, to Fort Mohave, Arizona, on the Colorado River. The plan was to have a rail stop at Cerro Gordo Landing, which was renamed Keeler (for mill owner and entrepreneur Julius M. Keeler), so that the great wealth of the Cerro Gordo mines could then be shipped from Keeler north to San Francisco, eliminating the route taken by boat and then pack train south to Los Angeles. Unfortunately, by the time the railroad was completed to Keeler in 1883,

The deteriorating Sierra Talc Company is Keeler's most prominent building. You can just barely read the word "Sierra" on the two-story middle structure.

The depot at Keeler served the Carson & Colorado Railroad. This is a building well worth restoring, or at least preserving.

A concrete wall in Keeler touts "Famous ABC Beer."

production at Cerro Gordo had ceased. When financier Darius O. Mills traveled along the route of his Carson & Colorado Railroad that same year for the end-of-track inspection, he looked at the empty scene at Keeler and somberly intoned, "Gentlemen, we either built it three hundred miles too long or three hundred years too soon." Mills sold the 293-mile-long white elephant to the Southern Pacific at a tremendous loss in 1900.

A tramway was constructed from Cerro Gordo to Keeler beginning in 1911, when zinc deposits were found in the old silver and lead mines, which resulted in a modest rebirth at Keeler and a legitimate purpose for the railroad. When the zinc operations shut down in the 1930s, the town headed toward ghost town status. The last train from Keeler left in April 1960, and the town truly was at the end of its line.

## WALKING AND DRIVING AROUND KEELER

Keeler has three fine buildings worth examining. The most prominent is the Sierra Talc Company plant, a favorite subject of artists. Unfortunately, the painted sign on the western face of the building has faded significantly since I first photographed it in the early 1980s.

West of the talc company is the Keeler School, obscured by foliage. A photo I have seen of students in front of the school is dated from the 1930s, so the school is obviously at least that old.

The two-story Carson & Colorado depot, which badly needs propping up or restoration, is the most intriguing building in town. At this writing, it is thoroughly boarded up, so one cannot even peer into its recesses.

To the east of the depot is an E Clampus Vitus historical plaque on Keeler's "end of the line" status, and south of the depot is a foundation with its western wall touting "Famous ABC Beer." I guess fame is relative.

Near the shore of Owens Dry Lake is the Keeler dry swimming pool, fenced, locked, and abandoned. I have seen a photo from the 1930s of bathing beauties posing on its deck.

Finally, on the north side of the highway just east of town stands the barren Keeler Cemetery.

## WHEN YOU GO

*Keeler is at the base of the Yellow Grade Road, the route to Cerro Gordo (see preceding entry), and 14.3 miles southeast of Lone Pine on California Highway 136.*

# 6

# SPIRITS

O F

# DEATH
# VALLEY

ITS NAME ALONE CAUSES MANY POTENTIAL VISITORS TO SHRINK IN FEAR: "Why on earth would I want to go *there*?" Death Valley likely received its ominous appellation from a member of the 1849 Bennett-Arcan party, who barely escaped the valley with their lives (except for one, Richard Culverwell, the first documented casualty there). That survivor is reported to have looked back ruefully and said, "Goodbye, Death Valley." Twelve years later a member of the Boundary Commission described it as a "vast and deep pit of many gloomy wonders."

Today's visitors to Death Valley will find a region of unspeakable beauty and astonishing variety, offering much more than barren flatlands.

In the previous chapter, you were near Mt. Whitney, the highest peak in the contiguous forty-eight states. In this chapter, you can visit the lowest point, at Badwater, standing at 282 feet below sea level. And if you go to Dante's View, a favorite stop in Death Valley, you can see, at least on the clearest days, both of those highest and lowest points from one spot.

Death Valley is the driest place in the United States and the hottest in the western hemisphere, so I suggest visiting in the spring when the valley floor has an unmatched profusion of wildflowers.

Baby gauge ore cars and flat car holding railroad ties stand above the town of Ryan.

A fifteen-stamp gold mill in Skidoo.

Whenever you go, make certain to reserve accommodations for your stay, inquire locally about the weather, and prepare yourself and your vehicle for the temperatures.

The sequence of sites in this chapter assumes that you are coming from Keeler, the last entry in the preceding chapter, and that you will be heading out of Death Valley at its southern end on your way to the following chapter.

To the ghost town enthusiast, the valley has several wonderful attractions, most notably Ryan, the best-preserved ghost town in the West. At this writing, it is closed to the public, but I am optimistic that it will eventually be open for limited visitation. Regardless, you will get an insider's view of Ryan in this chapter.

In addition to Ryan, your Death Valley visit will include a true ghost town with one magnificent mining structure, a historic borax processing plant, a former railroad community still hanging on, ten of the most beautiful charcoal kilns in the American West, and a town that was a swindler's scam

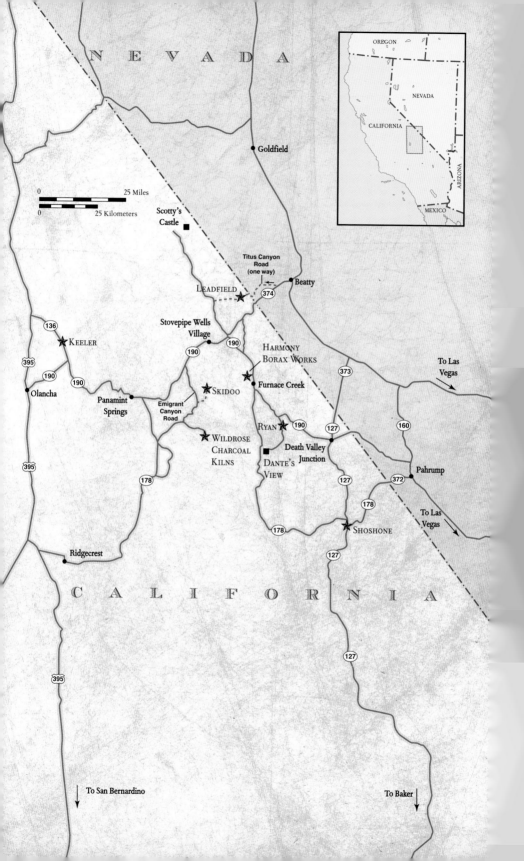

# SKIDOO

One of the most promising gold discoveries in Death Valley was made in 1906 when John L. Ramsey and John "One-Eyed" Thompson found primary deposits, dubbed the Gold Eagle, so vast that twenty-three claims were required to cover it. Bob Montgomery, who had made his fortune at Rhyolite (east of Death Valley in Nevada), bought out the two prospectors for $30,000 each. That was just as well for Ramsey and Thompson, because this was a mine that would require an enormous investment in order to make good. Montgomery spent $200,000 to build an iron pipeline traversing twenty-one miles from Birch Spring on Telescope Peak, the highest point in the Panamint Range, to bring water to the mine site. Water was essential for the townsite that would evolve, of course, but, just as importantly, it was required to process ore in the fifteen-stamp mill that began operation in 1907.

The town that grew at the mine was likely named by Bob Montgomery's wife, Winnie, who, when she heard that her husband had purchased twenty-three claims,

Skidoo's fifteen-stamp mill operated from 1907 until 1917 and processed an estimated $1.34 million in gold. *Photograph by Michael Moore*

reportedly said, "Twenty-three Skidoo," a then-popular expression meaning "skeedaddle," or to make a hasty exit. The U.S. Postal Service originally rejected the name Skidoo as frivolous but eventually relented, granting the post office in that name on April 1, 1907—April Fool's Day. Perhaps the federal government *does* have a sense of humor.

Skidoo was a rather sedate place for the most part because it was a one-owner company town. It featured its own newspaper, the *Skidoo News*; the members-only Tucki Club, featuring fine dining and elegant staterooms; and a telephone line that extended from Skidoo to Rhyolite, from which Montgomery and many of the miners came.

Skidoo was certainly not a sedate place one day in April 1908. It began when one of the town's favorite citizens, Jim Arnold, was shot and killed by Joe "Hootch" Simpson, one of Skidoo's most reviled denizens, allegedly because Arnold had kicked the drunken, surly Simpson. The sheriff apprehended Simpson, but an angry mob "relieved" the sheriff of his charge and summarily hanged him from a telephone pole. The *Skidoo News* crowed that other miscreants should "note the number, the stoutness, and the great convenience of the telephone poles, and reflect thereon."

On the next morning, Dr. Reginald Macdonald, who had apparently been treating Simpson with narcotics for syphilis, took two photographs of the deceased at a tent serving as a makeshift morgue, one on a table in the tent and another hanging from a tent beam. Those photos likely were taken after the corpse had been thrown down a shaft and then recovered by Dr. Macdonald, who wanted to examine Simpson's brain for signs of syphilis and consequently later beheaded the body. A story persists that the skull was kept by the doctor and passed to others over the years.

Skidoo's mines produced until 1917, yielding an estimated $1.34 million in gold. The town, which probably had a peak population of about seven hundred, lost its post office that same year. The pipeline was sold for scrap, terminating the only source of water for the moribund town.

## WALKING AND DRIVING AROUND SKIDOO

The Skidoo townsite offers little to the ghost town enthusiast. In fact, if it weren't for a park service sign and a few rusted cans, broken glass, and other debris, you could well drive past Skidoo altogether. When I first visited the site in 1981, there was no indication that anything else remained at the site. Because of the USGS topographic map of the area, I ventured beyond Skidoo, believing there was much more. And when *Southern California's Best Ghost Towns* was published in 1991, I sent my readers up around a back road to one of the most astonishing sights in the ghost town West.

On my most recent visit in 2010, the national park sign at Skidoo still doesn't tell you about what remains beyond the townsite, but there is at least an interpretive sign after you have followed my directions to a turnaround, have walked past a vehicle barrier, and have come to your destination: the remarkable Skidoo Mill.

I don't know whether my earlier book caused the turnaround, the barrier, and the sign, but I rather hope it did, because back roads people deserve to see this wonderful sight. Here's how you get there: From the Skidoo interpretive sign, follow the right fork of the road for 0.6 miles, where there is another fork. Go left as the road, which is passable for a passenger car but would be better with a truck, heads up onto the north side of a hill looking down into a draw. You will pass an adit on your left at 0.3 of a mile beyond the last fork. Park your vehicle at the turnaround beyond the adit and walk around the vehicle barrier to the west. The Skidoo Mill, which processed gold ore for a decade, will come gloriously into view. Please heed the signs that prohibit you from climbing onto the rickety structure.

## WHEN YOU GO

*If you are coming from Keeler (the final entry in the preceding chapter), drive 55.6 miles east on California Highway 190 into Death Valley until you reach the turnoff onto Emigrant Canyon Road. From there, proceed 9.4 miles south to a dirt road with an historical sign directing the way to Skidoo. The townsite is 7 miles beyond the turnoff on a road for which I recommend a truck, although I have seen passenger vehicles at Skidoo. For specific directions to the Skidoo Mill, consult the paragraph above.*

*If you are coming from Death Valley, the turnoff to Emigrant Canyon Road is 9 miles west of Stovepipe Wells Village. Then follow the directions immediately above.*

# THE WILDROSE CHARCOAL KILNS

The Wildrose Charcoal Kilns are a testament to the tenacity and perseverance that early miners demonstrated in their quest for mineral wealth. When rich lead ore was discovered at the Modock (later Modoc) Mine in 1875 on the western fringe of the Panamint Valley, a smelter was required to process the ore for efficient transporting, since smelted ore no longer has the heavy, and expensive, detritus of milled ore. The problem was that there was no forest near the Modock to supply the wood needed for a charcoal-fired smelter.

The solution was found a full twenty-five miles away, over very hilly terrain, up in the Panamint Mountains in a piñon forest at an elevation of about 7,000 feet. In 1877, at the mouth of Wildrose Canyon, Chinese laborers erected ten "beehive" kilns, designed by Swiss engineers, which were used to convert wood to charcoal. (For a more complete explanation of the process, see The Cottonwood Charcoal Kilns entry, page 164.)

A modest town of about a hundred people bloomed at the Wildrose site, with a store, a boardinghouse, and a blacksmith shop. The kilns only produced fuel for the Modock smelter for about a year and a half, when the mines at Modock closed.

The beautifully constructed Wildrose Charcoal Kilns were only in use for about eighteen months.

The lower entrance in each Wildrose Canyon kiln allowed for the initial stacking of wood. A higher rear entrance was used for the final stacking. *Photograph by Michael Moore*

## WALKING AROUND THE WILDROSE CHARCOAL KILNS

I have taken two friends to these kilns to see if I am simply too enthusiastic about them, as I am a confessed kiln fanatic. On both occasions, once in 1981 and again in 2010, the friends remarked: "Wow. Oh, wow" (1981) and "These are remarkable, simply remarkable" (2010). It is hard for me to believe that you will be any less awed. Be sure to examine the kilns' craftsmanship inside and out. Look west across the various mountain ranges and try to imagine the difficulty of transporting the resultant charcoal twenty-five miles to the Modock Mine's smelter. Your appreciation for the nineteenth-century teamster and his mules will soar.

### WHEN YOU GO

*From the turnoff to Skidoo, head south on Emigrant Canyon Road for 10.5 miles to the Wildrose Ranger Station and Campground. The kilns are 7 miles beyond that turnoff on a road that climbs high into Wildrose Canyon and is paved for all but the last mile.*

# THE HARMONY BORAX WORKS

Prospectors combed all over Death Valley looking for the next big strike. They were encouraged by the deep variations of colors in the mountain ranges, variations that often mean the presence of precious metals. Despite all the searching (and occasional strikes at Skidoo, Panamint City, and the Keane Wonder Mine), it was more mundane elements that brought genuine mineral wealth to the valley. The primary discovery was borax, which has been used for centuries in pottery glazes and metal-working fluxes, and more recently in the production of fiberglass. It also has many household uses such as a shampoo, a cleanser, a deodorant, and a water softener.

The borax boom began in Death Valley in 1881 when visitors to valley residents Aaron Winters and his wife, Rosie, suspecting that the flats contained borax, showed Winters a simple test for it. Out on those flats Winters applied the test and cried out, "She burns green, Rosie! We're rich, by God!"

Winters sent samples to William T. Coleman in San Francisco, who paid Winters $20,000 for the rights to the deposits he owned. This particular borax was ulexite, also known as "cottonball" for its fluffy appearance. In 1882, a year after the discovery, the Harmony Borax Works was in production. Chinese workers gathered the borax from the nearby marshy deposits while Indians cut wood to fuel a boiler. The boiler heated large vats with a solution of carbonate and water that hardened to crystal form on iron rods within the vats. The crystals were dried and loaded onto wagons pulled by eight-mule teams to take the borax to a railhead

The remains of the Harmony Borax Works date from the 1882, the earliest borax production in Death Valley.

The famous twenty-mule team teams pulled two wagons filled with borax followed by a trailing water wagon.

at Mojave, 165 miles and ten days away across some of the driest, hottest, and most forbidding terrain on earth. Increasing volumes of borax eventually led to larger wagons and, consequently, to the use of the now-famous twenty-mule teams.

The operation at Harmony closed in 1888, after only five effective years of production, because a more easily mined form of borax, named Colemanite in honor of William T. Coleman, was discovered in the mountains above the marshes.

## WALKING AROUND THE HARMONY BORAX WORKS

When you leave your vehicle at the parking lot, you walk up a short path that elevates just enough to have a dramatic view of the borax works, the flats below, and a three-wagon ensemble that once was pulled by those famous twenty-mule teams. It is a sight that encapsulates Death Valley better than any spot I know: you see the beauty, the barrenness, the original industry, and the historic means of transportation all in one view.

The works themselves consist of the old boiler, vats, adobe walls, and various relics of the operation. You can also take a walk down into the flats to see where the Chinese workers gathered the "cottonball." Here you can read interpretive signs to expand your understanding of this interesting process.

## WHEN YOU GO

*The Harmony Borax Works is 1.3 miles north of the Furnace Creek Visitor Center on California Highway 190. Furnace Creek is 26 miles southeast of Stovepipe Wells Village.*

## THE DEATH VALLEY VISITORS CENTER,
## THE FURNACE CREEK RANCH BORAX MUSEUM, AND OLD DINAH

The center of the action in Death Valley lies immediately south of the Harmony Borax Works. The Death Valley Visitors Center, closed in 2010 but completely rebuilt and scheduled to reopen in the spring of 2012, is the place where you pay your entrance fee. (This is, after all, a national park.) But this is also the place to see extensive displays on every imaginable aspect of Death Valley like flora and fauna, history, and geology. The rangers can also provide details about weather and road conditions, and lodging and camping availability.

Furnace Creek Ranch is south of the visitors center. Within the grounds of the compound are restaurants, a motel, a general store, the area's post office, and other establishments. But for the ghost town enthusiast, the Borax Museum is the place to see. This free museum features ore samples, miners' tools, and information on the twenty-mule teams. The outdoor section of the museum offers mining equipment and an assortment of carts and wagons. In the back corner stands a narrow-gauge Baldwin 2-8-0 locomotive that was used to haul borax from Ryan (see entry, page 190) to the Tonopah and Tidewater main line at Death Valley Junction.

Old Dinah, another Death Valley vehicle of note, stands at the entrance to Furnace Creek Ranch. Old Dinah was a steam traction train that operated at Calico (see page 212) but was last used in Death Valley. It was supposed to replace twenty-mule team wagon trains, but it handled poorly on hills and dug itself into soft sand. Not only were Teamsters and their mules not replaced, they actually gained added employment pulling Old Dinah out of trouble. It died of a ruptured boiler in 1909 trying to ascend Daylight Pass on the way to Beatty and was left to rust until it was brought, two decades later, to be put on display at Furnace Creek Ranch.

When I most recently saw Old Dinah, the steam-powered traction train that was a dismal failure in Death Valley, the contraption was surrounded by automobiles. I took this photograph in 1981, but it looks much the same today.

# LEADFIELD

Sometimes the journey is more important than the destination, as is the case with Leadfield. Though a minor site, accessing Leadfield entails one of the loveliest imaginable drives—you'll head from high desert into the varied colors and geologic upheaval of the Grapevine Mountains, taking dramatic twists and turns on a one-way road—and the drive beyond the tiny townsite into Titus Canyon is one of the signature experiences in Death Valley. Named for Morris Titus, a young mining engineer who died on the Valley floor, this slot canyon is so narrow at points that it seems as if your truck will touch the walls on both sides. At the end of the canyon, the portal into Death Valley itself provides an unforgettable view.

But let's go back to Leadfield. When you leave your vehicle at the small parking area and walk to the sparse remains of Leadfield—three corrugated buildings, one a falsefront; a miner's dugout; and a couple of adits and waste dumps—you will be standing in the middle of a colossal swindle.

C. C. (Courtney Chauncy) Julian certainly knew how to profit from a loser. His Julian Petroleum Company, known as "Julian Pete," was supposed, according to C. C., to "make that Standard Oil crowd turn flip-flops." It was Julian Pete that flopped, taking stockholders for a ride. In 1926, he began to entice investors for his fledgling company Western Lead, named for spectacular lead pockets he claimed were ready to be tapped in the Grapevine Mountains of Death Valley. In reality, the only pockets Julian tapped where those of the gullible suckers who invested in his scam.

Julian, it is suspected, brought in lead ore from elsewhere to salt the canyon. Then he took out full-page ads in newspapers touting the investment opportunities. He distributed handbills depicting lead-filled steamers negotiating the Amargosa River. That is true chutzpah: if you visit Beatty, Nevada, the closest town east of Leadfield, be sure to notice the raging Amargosa, one of the longest *underground* rivers in the world. He then topped off the ruse by inviting 340 "lucky" potential investors to join him on a chartered train from Los Angeles to Beatty, where they were ushered into more than ninety waiting automobiles to escort them to Leadfield, followed by about eight hundred other "less fortunate" folk who had to provide their own transportation. It was a convincing gambit. The town blossomed to a population of about three hundred hopeful citizens, and hundreds more purchased stock. As historian W. A. Chalfant wryly observed, Leadfield had all the qualities of a successful mining town—except paying ore.

Leadfield's meager remains stand near Titus Canyon, one of Death Valley's most beautiful spots. *Photograph by Michael Moore*

When no mining equipment materialized to begin operating, when no activity whatsoever ensued, citizens slowly began to realize they had been duped. Arthur R. Benton wrote in an article for *Desert Magazine* that he and a friend wandered into Leadfield, having mistakenly driven their Model T Ford the wrong way up Titus Canyon. He reported that the good people of Leadfield were in a decidedly ugly mood.

C. C. Julian reaped a reported $900,000 windfall on his Leadfield scam (that's more than $11 million in today's dollars) and managed two more swindles in Arizona and Oklahoma before hastily jumping bail and exiting the country in 1933 for Shanghai. It was there, penniless and fearing extradition back to the United States., that he committed suicide a year later. He was buried in a pauper's grave.

## WHEN YOU GO

*From the Death Valley Visitors Center at Furnace Creek, go north on California Highway 190 for 10.9 miles, where a well-marked cutoff takes you northeast for 10 miles toward Beatty, Nevada. Continue northeast by taking a right turn when that cutoff meets Daylight Pass Road, which will become Nevada Highway 374 when you enter that state. Continue for 13 miles from the cutoff, where a clearly marked turn sends you toward Titus Canyon (and back into California). Leadfield is 16 miles from that turnoff and about an hour away. When you leave the townsite, expect to take about 40 minutes for the 12-mile journey to the floor of Death Valley, longer if you pause many times, as I have on my three visits, to be entranced by the scenery. The road is recommended for four-wheel-drive vehicles. I have driven it in a two-wheel-drive truck, but I felt much more comfortable with a four-wheel-drive, high-clearance vehicle. The road is occasionally closed, as for several miles it follows a normally dry wash.*

*Note: At the point you turn off the highway to go to Leadfield, you'll be very near one of Nevada's better ghost towns, Rhyolite. For more information on that site, consult my book* Ghost Towns of the Mountain West, *also from Voyageur Press.*

# RYAN

Ryan is very likely America's most complete ghost town. It has never truly been abandoned; caretakers have spared it from most of the vandalism and looting common at unguarded sites. Maintenance work has continued over the decades, so, although Ryan certainly shows its age, it is not falling apart. It is a ghost town rarity and a treasure, unique in the United States.

The Pacific Coast Borax Company began operations at the Lila C. Mine in 1890. The camp that developed at the mine was called Ryan, in honor of John Ryan, manager of the company. Peak production took place at the Lila C. from 1907 until 1914, with more than $8 million in colemanite borax extracted, making the mine richer than all other Death Valley mines combined.

When the Lila C. apparently played out in 1914, Pacific Coast Borax relocated its headquarters to Devar (an approximate acronym for Death Valley Railroad, which carried the borate ore). A 1910 topographic map of the area identifies the community as "Devair." The spelling variation is immaterial, since the place was renamed Ryan not long after the original Ryan was abandoned. One train per day ran from Death Valley Junction, heading northwest and then looping around to proceed south to Ryan, where the line terminated. The train brought water in the morning and took out ore in the afternoon. Passengers (and the mail) took the route separately in a 1912 Cadillac touring car with flanged wheels. A two-foot-wide "baby gauge" railroad, built in 1915–1916, extended south from the town to the Grandview and the Lizzy V. Oakley Mines. By 1919, the baby gauge extended farther south to the Widow Mine, when new ore bodies were found in that heretofore underperforming mine.

This was a highly successful operation: The mines at the new Ryan combined for a yield of over two hundred tons of ore per day, about double what the Lila C. had produced in its best days. A mill at Death Valley Junction, which reduced the ore for shipment, ran twenty-four hours a day, seven days a week. Death Valley Junction was a stop on the Tonopah & Tidewater Railroad, which took the ore south to Ludlow. (For more on that railroad, see Shoshone, the next entry in this chapter.)

The original Devar, or Devair, had been a hodgepodge of dilapidated structures primarily brought from other sites, but all that changed when Major Julian Boyd, a former Australian army officer, was installed as the new manager at Ryan in 1920. He basically set fire to the mangy town and called upon the company to erect fireproof dormitories and a dozen houses for the staff. He also brought a Catholic church by rail from Rhyolite to Ryan to serve as the recreation hall and movie theater. In addition, he added a one-room school to what became a model company town. These improvements made him enormously popular with the workers at Ryan and also gave us the structures that still stand today.

Production at Ryan flourished for seven more years. In 1920, the same year as the rebuilding of Ryan, workers removing old timbers from the Lila C., inactive since 1914, found an entirely new ore body when the old works caved in.

In 1927, however, Ryan was closed when huge borate deposits were found in Boron, east of Mojave. Boron has been the major source of borax in America ever since and today supplies nearly 40 percent of the global demand for refined borates. But it is worth remembering that Death Valley borax mines were enormously profitable, producing more than $30 million (that's about $389 million in today's dollars) in ore in their thirty-seven years of operation, far more than any other mines in Death Valley or the nearby Amargosa Valley.

Ryan had a modest second life after the mining operations closed. The bunkhouses, the remodeled hospital, and the dining rooms became the Death

The former combination post office and company store at Ryan stands to the left of what became the "lobby" of the Death Valley View Hotel after mining operations ceased.

Ryan's recreation hall and movie theater was a Catholic church in Rhyolite, Nevada, before it was brought by rail to its present location.

A view from the former choir loft shows that Ryan's recreation hall still has a usable stage, complete with footlights.

Valley View Hotel, which offered less expensive accommodations than the Furnace Creek Inn, which Pacific Coast Borax opened in 1927 and which remains a lovely, luxurious resort to this day. Ryan's Death Valley View Hotel also offered competition to another reasonable hotel twenty-eight miles northwest of Furnace Creek at Stovepipe Wells Village, which had opened in 1926 as the valley's first resort. At an elevation of 3,040 feet, the temperature at Death Valley View on hot days was also about twenty degrees cooler than at the hotels on the Valley floor.

Death Valley View Hotel guests, who arrived on a self-propelled, gasoline-powered, Brill railroad car, could also take a seven-mile ride on Ryan's baby gauge railroad for only a dollar. (For more information about that Brill railroad car, which has been restored and still runs, see page 157.) A tennis court was even added to the facility to increase the guests' enjoyment. But when the Death Valley Railroad was discontinued in 1930, the hotel was finished as well, because the railroad was the lifeline for the Death Valley View. The railroad had delivered Ryan's water since 1914, and without that delivery, the hotel was out of business.

The rise in the popularity (and reliability) of the automobile brought more and more tourists to Death Valley, which became a destination people sought at least in part to be able to say they had done it—perhaps the way the ALCAN Highway, from Canada to Alaska, is viewed today. And as the tourists explored the attractions of Death Valley, Ryan, closed to the public, became a ghost town perched high on the side of a mountain, tantalizing but out of reach to the travelers on the road to Dante's View.

## WALKING AROUND RYAN

I first saw Ryan in December 1981 and gazed in awe at the town in the distance and with frustration at the gate that barred entry. I was able, nevertheless, to get a reasonable view of the town through a telephoto camera lens and binoculars and included the photographs in my third book, *Southern California's Best Ghost Towns*, published in 1990.

If that is as close as you have permission to go, here is what you can see, starting from the left (the north end): the recreation hall and movie theater (the church brought from Rhyolite), followed by two two-story dormitories, with a small steam plant between and just below them. Behind the dorms, which were also called "bunkhouses" at the time, is the two-story hospital.

The chalkboards of the school feature hundreds of names, many of them of San Jose State University geology students who came on field trips to Ryan.

Above and behind the hospital is a derelict residence (known as House Four). Then, on the same level as the hospital's second floor, are Houses Three, Two, and One. High above House Three is the town's water tank. The rest of Ryan is obscured by hills.

I was, fortunately, able to get much, much closer. Imagine my joy when an official of Rio Tinto Minerals (see Acknowledgments, page 228), the successor to the Pacific Coast Borax Company, asked me after a Nevada historical conference in 2007 if I would like to visit Ryan. I wanted to go right then, but I had to wait until my next trip to Death Valley, which occurred in January 2008. On that visit I met Ryan's caretaker (again, see Acknowledgments, page 228), who invited me back several times. On my first visit, he took me on a basic tour and then allowed me to explore on my own. This was ghost town heaven. On my second visit, a year later, I could hardly believe it: I was sleeping in one of the houses I had seen through the binoculars more than twenty-seven years before. I visited Ryan five times, the last in December 2010. Rio Tinto, the parent company that owned Ryan, was planning to donate the land and buildings to a nonprofit agency, along with funds to restore, preserve, and protect this historic property for future generations. At this writing, that donation has not yet taken place.

Ryan looks like what it was—a company town. The buildings are very much the same, all white with green trim and metal roofs. What the structures lack in individuality is compensated by the enchanting sum total of the whole complex. There are some missing residences that were below and across from the school, but overall the town is intact. Considering that Ryan effectively closed for good in 1930, that's remarkable.

The most architecturally creative building is the former recreation hall and movie theater, which as previously mentioned, was not constructed at Ryan but at Rhyolite. But even it has been brought into the uniformity of the other buildings, except for its church-style lancet windows, which lost their stained glass after being moved to Ryan. The hall has footlights on the stage (which was added at Ryan), a roll-down curtain mechanism, and, in the rear, a wooden gate across a steep staircase that goes up to a choir loft. If the building had a spire in Rhyolite, it has none here.

Next door to the recreation hall, the hospital offers a tribute to the television program *Death Valley Days* on its second floor. The program ran from 1952 to

Ryan's schoolhouse stands in the foreground. Houses Four, Three, and Two stand from left to right in the background. You can also see the schoolyard's swing, pivoting seesaw, and merry-go-round.

1975, including a hosting stint by future president Ronald Reagan. The longest-running host was known as "The Old Ranger," played by actor Stanley Andrews, who is acknowledged in a restored room in the northwestern corner complete with monogrammed towels and various borax products and memorabilia, including the periodical "Old Ranger Yarns."

In many unrestored dorm and hospital rooms, curtains hang, sinks are in place, and dilapidated bedsprings are ready for mattresses. But the sinks don't work, and the showers and toilets in the communal bathrooms are inoperable.

When I visited, the three livable residential buildings variously served as guesthouses, the main kitchen, and the caretaker's home.

Those are the only buildings you can see from down at the road in front of the barricade. Among others on the site is the schoolhouse, which is the first building you pass as you enter Ryan. It features a small bell tower (with its bell), and desks, chairs, and chalkboards inside. Outside are three pieces of playground equipment: a swing hanging from a wooden framework, a merry-go-round, and something I have never seen elsewhere—a seesaw that also pivots, which brings a whole new dimension to the experience.

Beyond the school, the entry road ends on a level spot that was the old railroad grade entering Ryan from the north. It now looks like the town's main street. At the south end of that "street" are three buildings. On the left is the former company store and post office, now a machine shop. In the center stands a building that originally had two dining rooms and a kitchen. When the Death Valley View Hotel opened, one dining room was converted into the hotel's lobby. That lobby, featuring a river rock fireplace, contains wonderful memorabilia, including photographs and Pacific Coast Borax Company posters. The adjoining dining room was the restaurant of the hotel, and beyond that is the kitchen, which still has its large icebox, stove, and steel counters.

West of the lobby is a two-story warehouse that contains all sorts of equipment, like train wheels and pulleys. Also stored in the warehouse are sets of dishes waiting to serve patrons who will never return. Six bedrooms are on the second floor of the warehouse and two more are on the first floor; posted material hints that perhaps they were the rooms of the kitchen staff.

South of these three structures, down in a draw, stands the powerhouse for the operation, which had three oil-fueled generators: one for the mining operation, one for the town, and one to be used as a backup.

Ryan's recreation hall stands in the background as seen through the front porch of House Three. Also visible on the left is the second floor of the former hospital.

On a hill east of the store/post office are some ore cars of the baby gauge railroad. In a tunnel nearby sits the turn-of-the-twentieth-century Plymouth locomotive and its baby gauge tourist cars, still in operating condition. The tracks themselves head south from town, but slides and later bulldozer work have rendered the line unusable at this writing.

Just north of town, on a lower level, a group of miners' homes called "Copenhagen Row" once stood. All that is left are rock foundations and debris of the cabins, which predated the 1920 reconstruction of Ryan. About 2.5 miles north of town, along the old Death Valley Railroad grade, is a tiny cemetery with evidence of six graves, including one for a German who called himself John Smith (actually Johann Schmidt, perhaps?), who is believed to have committed suicide in 1924 by blowing himself up with dynamite.

If you can visit Ryan no other way, you can view it as it appeared in the 1950s in at least three episodes of the old television series *Death Valley Days*, which are now available on DVD. Of those episodes, "Million Dollar Wedding" (filmed in 1955) shows more of the town than the others, including the recreation hall (used as the church for the wedding), the company store porch, the bell tower of the school (which we are cleverly led to believe is atop the "church"), and a special treat: the baby gauge railroad in operation. It also shows a house across from the school that no longer exists.

Ryan was also used for the opening scene of *Spartacus*, with Kirk Douglas. The buildings were kept carefully out of camera range, but, if you look carefully, you can see, as the camera pans that early scene, the old Death Valley Railroad grade extending anachronistically in the background. *Spartacus* was released in 1960, and by that time some of the baby gauge rails that were used in "Million Dollar Wedding" had been removed.

## WHEN YOU GO

*Ryan is southeast of Furnace Creek Ranch. From the ranch, take California Highway 190 for 12 miles southeast to the turnoff to Dante's View. The dirt road to the barricade at the foot of Ryan is about 2.5 miles on the left from that turnoff. You will have a clear view of the town. Do not proceed beyond that barricade unless you have been given permission to do so.*

# SHOSHONE

When I was doing field research in the 1980s for *Southern California's Best Ghost Towns*, I visited Shoshone and mistakenly dismissed it. Fortunately, when I returned in 2010, I stayed overnight and took a longer look. This is an unusual town with a colorful history that is well worth visiting and exploring.

Shoshone ("shuh-*show*-nee") was originally merely a siding along the Tonopah & Tidewater Railroad. The railroad's name was a monument to thinking big. Tonopah, Nevada, was a booming gold town in the 1900s, and the Tidewater part of the moniker referred to a vague seaport area near San Diego. The line didn't quite live up to its name in either direction: Its southern terminus was in Ludlow, east of Barstow, where construction on the line running north began in 1905. Its northern terminus, reached two years later, was in Gold Center, just south of Beatty, Nevada. Considering the lofty goals of the Tonopah & Tidewater name, the distance of the line, 167 miles, seems rather meager. Although the railroad never turned a profit itself, it served its primary purpose well: it was constructed mainly to get Death Valley borax to processing plants and from those plants to national and world markets. That was important because the T & T was owned by Francis Marion "Borax" Smith, president of the Pacific Coast Borax Company.

Shoshone, which was named for an indigenous Indian tribe, went from a siding and water stop to an actual town in 1910 when Ralph Jacobus "Dad" Fairbanks moved a series of buildings from the dying town of Greenwater, northwest of Shoshone, down to land he leased at the Shoshone siding. He and his wife, Celesta (I have also seen her name spelled "Celeste" and "Celestia"), were the founding citizens of the new community. Fairbanks built a small station with rudimentary facilities for passengers and crew of the Tonopah & Tidewater.

In that same year, Charles G. "Charlie" Brown also came from Greenwater, where he had been both an engineer and a deputy sheriff, to Shoshone, where he married Fairbank's daughter Stella. The Fairbanks and Brown families would eventually form the backbone of the small community.

In 1916, Dad Fairbanks had an experience that would change Shoshone's history. As he told the story, Fairbanks came upon a woman in the Shoshone Indian camp washing her hair in a substance that looked like mud (but was actually clay) mixed with water in a consistency much like buttermilk. When she

Shoshone miners carved residences out of caliche cliffs in the 1920s.

completed her task, her hair was not only clean but also soft, with a glossy sheen. She told Fairbanks where she found the material, and he staked a claim. That material became known as filter clay, which eventually was used in refineries to clean or to clarify heavy oils. He sold his claim to the Associated Oil Company for an undisclosed sum. All Fairbanks would reveal was that "It was a tidy fortune—a comfortable stake for Dad Fairbanks and Mother for the rest of their days."

Charlie and Stella Brown, Fairbanks' son-in-law and daughter, lived in other mining towns for several years, but in 1920 they returned with their children to Shoshone to join her parents in various business ventures, including a restaurant that Charlie and Stella ran in a building that still stands in the small community.

Dad Fairbanks and Charlie Brown watched as Death Valley became more popular as a tourist destination. Since Shoshone was the southern portal to the Valley, they decided to capitalize on their location and in 1925 began building a four-room motel, the Old Timer's Inn, completed the next year. Their foresight was well deserved, and they added and remodeled cabins from nearby abandoned mining camps as the need arose.

Brown made a lasting legacy within Death Valley itself. To attract more tourists, the governors of California and Nevada wanted a viewpoint from which to see the majesty and scope of the valley. They had initially settled upon a lookout from the Chloride Cliff Mine, high in the Funeral Mountains (which, incidentally, I have seen—it *is* a stunning view). Charlie, when asked, said he knew a better location, and he escorted the governors' party to a place that was ultimately selected, the now-famous Dante's View. Brown even made money on the decision, for it was he who graded the road south to the overlook from Furnace Creek Wash.

On Sunday, March 26, 1926, the citizens of Shoshone were treated to one of the most memorable days in the community's history. The town had received advance word that C. C. Julian's "Julian Special" train (see Leadfield, page 188), with its dual locomotives and fifteen elegant varnished wooden coaches, would pass through Shoshone in the early hours of morning. At 1:45 a.m., when the Julian Special came through Shoshone, the entire town lined the tracks to see the spectacle of 340 "lucky" prospective investors on their way to what would become one of the West's most elaborate and successful financial fleecings.

The Fairbanks and Brown General Store, moved to Shoshone in about 1920, now serves as the Shoshone Museum.

Shoshone's prosperity began to wane when the Tonopah & Tidewater ran its last train in 1940. Borax was no longer being shipped from Death Valley, and trucks took over both the short- and long-haul transportation of goods in the Death Valley area. The town, however, has remained a natural stopping point for travelers passing through Death Valley and Baker (California), as well as Pahrump and Las Vegas (Nevada).

## WALKING AND DRIVING AROUND SHOSHONE

The logical place to start your tour is the Shoshone Museum, located in the heart of town in what appears to be an old gas station. That's because it was, along with being the Fairbanks and Brown General Store. The building itself is a museum piece, as it is the oldest structure in town. Dad Fairbanks moved this building, as he did so many others, from Greenwater, where it was erected in 1906 as a union hall and later served as a hospital. Fairbanks first moved it to Zabriskie Point, another T & T railroad stop five miles south of Shoshone. He moved it again in about 1920 to this location to become the general store. The building served in that capacity, as well as a post office and social center, until 1949, when a new general store was built across the street (where it still stands). A rusting 1937 Chevrolet stands waiting for fuel at a pump that announces that regular gas sells for 39.9¢ per gallon. I figure that price is frozen in time from the pump's last year of service, probably 1949. Lest we get too nostalgic for a price like that, the Consumer Price Inflation Index suggests that 39.9¢ in 1949 approaches $4.00 today—which is approximately what you will pay at the pump in Shoshone at this writing.

Widely available in town is a walking tour map of historic Shoshone. With that in hand, you can visit all of its twenty-seven spots with confidence. I'll just mention a few, including, immediately north of the museum, the Amargosa Conservancy, which is located in the home of pioneers Charlie and Stella Brown. The residence was built in 1926 as ordered from a Sears, Roebuck catalogue. And next door to the museum to the south is the Crowbar Café and Saloon, originally called the Red Buggy, which dates from the late 1930s. Next door to the south is what is known as "The Adobe Building," now the Inyo County Sheriff's Office, which once served as the restaurant run by Charlie and Stella Brown.

The most unusual place to explore is Dublin Gulch. Miners in the 1920s carved a series of "residences," actually man-made caves, into the caliche clay embankments in the gulch. The name may have come from Joe Vollmer, who had lived in a Dublin Gulch in Butte, Montana, prior to his arrival in Shoshone. Vollmer was known, especially during Prohibition, for his high-quality homemade beer. He had arrived in Shoshone in 1922 and worked for the Allied Petroleum Company, which was extracting Dad Fairbanks' filter clay discovery. (I am guessing that Allied Petroleum bought the claim from the Associated Oil Company, which paid Dad Fairbanks, although I found no concrete evidence of that.)

Today the Dublin Gulch dwellings, more than a dozen in number, are vacant, the last resident having left in the 1970s. But you will enjoy walking around the gulch and peering into the rooms, some of which have niches (perhaps for religious figurines), doors with transoms, various stovepipes and vent holes, and even a garage.

At the mouth of the gulch stands the Shoshone Cemetery, which includes the graves of Charlie and Stella Brown, who died in 1963 and 1970, respectively. Incidentally, Dad and Celesta Fairbanks, the original pioneers of the community, are not buried in Shoshone. They moved on to Baker, south of Shoshone, and later to Santa Paula. As far as I can determine, Celesta died in 1938, after which Dad moved to Hollywood, where he died in 1942 or 1943 (records differ).

Another, more elaborate caliche dwelling, known as the Castle in Clay, was excavated by Harvey Rutledge. It stands on the north side of the road at a point 0.6 of a mile east of Shoshone.

## WHEN YOU GO

*From Furnace Creek Ranch, drive 29 miles east on California 190 to Death Valley Junction. Then turn south on California Highway 127 and drive 27.2 miles to Shoshone. From Ryan, return north on the road to Dante's View to California Highway 190, turn right toward Death Valley Junction and follow the directions above.*

# 7

# GHOST TOWNS

## OF THE

# MOJAVE DESERT

THE MOJAVE DESERT PRESENTED CALIFORNIA PIONEERS TWO CHALLENGES—to mine it and to cross it. Mining occurred at places like Calico, Randsburg, and Tropico, all sites in this chapter. Even more memorable in the state's history, however, are the treks across the desert by mule teams going to and from the bonanzas at Cerro Gordo and in Death Valley.

The ghost towns in this chapter are, I will admit, not as spectacular as many in this book. But each has its allure. Kelso features a remarkably beautiful restored depot. Goffs has an interesting schoolhouse. Calico is a tourist town with an historic heart. Randsburg offers an excellent main street with several photogenic buildings. The Tropico Gold Mine, although closed to the public, is an artist's dream as it perches dramatically on a hill. Willow Springs features several faithfully restored buildings. And Llano is a ghost town purist's delight: there you can discover remnants of an unusual community that thousands of automobile drivers overlook every day.

All sites in this chapter are along paved roads, but some of the towns remain in isolated areas. Please remember that the desert can be deadly to the unwary; be prepared and take proper precautions on those back road journeys.

Most of the students at the school in Calico were the children of the town's merchants, because very few of the miners had families.

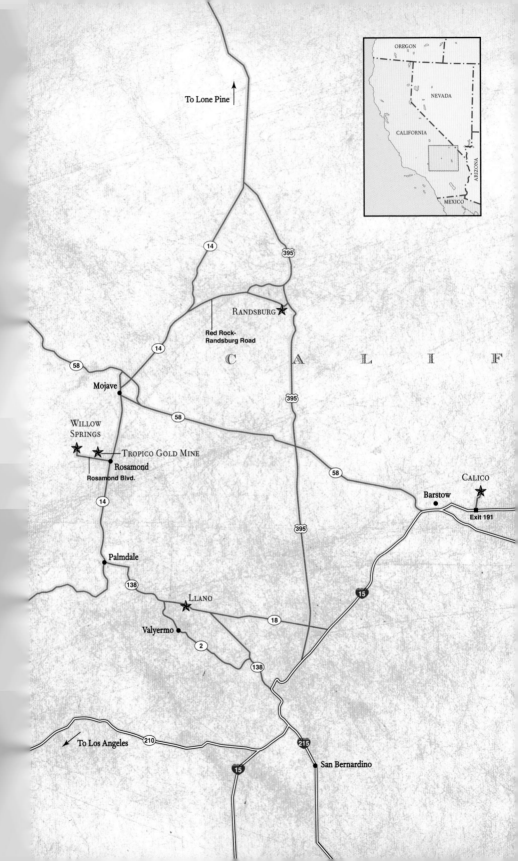

To Lone Pine

OREGON
NEVADA
CALIFORNIA
ARIZONA
MEXICO

14    395

RANDSBURG ✦
Red Rock-
Randsburg Road

C  A  L  I  F

14

58   Mojave

58

395

WILLOW
SPRINGS ✦    ✦
TROPICO GOLD MINE
Rosamond
Rosamond Blvd.

58

CALICO ✦
Barstow
Exit 191

14

Palmdale

395

15

138   LLANO ✦

18

Valyermo

2

138

To Los Angeles   210   215

15   San Bernardino

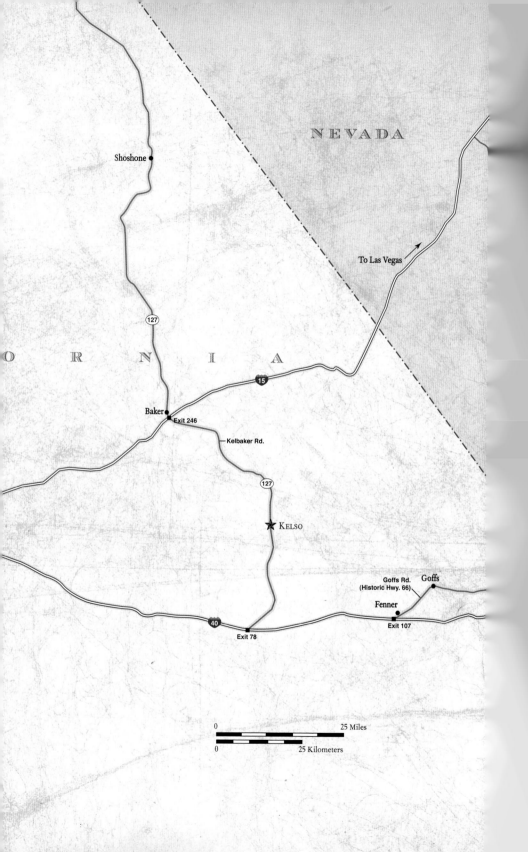

# KELSO

Kelso is one of the most unlikely visions in this book. No matter which direction you come from, you traverse wide open spaces of the Mojave Desert until, in the distance, you will see an unlikely outpost—an elegant, two-story depot dominating a tiny town the way a cathedral dominates a small European hamlet.

Kelso came into being because it was a logical spot for a siding along a rail line that extended, by 1905, from Salt Lake City to San Pedro, an important seaport south of Los Angeles. Originally known as Siding #16, the name for the spot was drawn from a hat containing the names of three workers, including John Kelso. The location was ideal because Kelso was situated near the bottom of a long grade heading northeast, so helper locomotives of the San Pedro, Los Angeles & Salt Lake Railroad (partly owned by and later absorbed into the Union Pacific Railroad) could be stored there to assist trains going up the grade. It was also ideal because there was a reliable source of water, crucial to steam engines, at a spring in the nearby Providence Mountains.

Discoveries of gold and silver deposits in those same mountains spurred growth in what became known as the Kelso District, adding to the importance of the growing community along the tracks.

Kelso's graceful, Spanish Mission–style depot was erected in 1925, replacing a much more modest station built in 1905, in part to compete with the elegant Harvey Houses that had been constructed along the competing Santa Fe route. Passengers had become accustomed to the luxury of the Santa Fe, and the Union Pacific had to respond in kind.

During World War II, Kelso became important to the war effort when iron ore was discovered in the area, especially at Kaiser Steel's Vulcan Mine. The ore from that mine helped to build the "Liberty Ships" of World War II. At that time, Kelso had burgeoned to a community of more than 2,000 citizens and the depot became the town's center, serving as the site for dances, church services, Christmas parties, and even trials.

Although many freight trains still pass through Kelso daily, the last passenger train came through in 1997. The Vulcan Mine closed in 1946, and when diesel engines replaced steam locomotives, the water stop was unnecessary. A concerned group of citizens formed to save the depot from demolition in the 1980s, and the federal government's Bureau of Land Management, which already oversaw much of the land in the area, took ownership. Eventually the National Park Service took over the depot, and restoration of the magnificent building was begun in 2002, reopening to the public in 2005.

Kelso's 1925 Spanish Mission–style depot, like many along the Union Pacific Railroad, were built to compete with the Harvey House depots of the rival Santa Fe Railroad.

## WALKING AROUND KELSO

The primary attraction today is, of course, the depot, with its long brick platform and its elms and palms offering shade from the desert sun. Across the street from the parking area is the combination former post office and L. J. Packard General Store. East of that building is the old schoolhouse and teacherage, which are slated for restoration, and, beyond them, a wooden structure with a Quonset-style roof. Across the tracks, south of the depot, stand some modern buildings and mobile homes.

You will want to take a leisurely tour of the depot. The telegraph room features an old telegraph key, a vintage typewriter, and various rubber stamps for documents. The second floor is a museum, with displays, maps, and memorabilia. The basement has a wonderful model of Kelso in the 1940s, with the town's buildings and railroad layout, which gives you a real sense of the size of Kelso at its zenith. One of the most appealing elements of the depot is The Beanery, an operating lunch counter restored to its 1924 appearance.

### WHEN YOU GO

*Kelso is 34.5 miles southeast of Baker, which is 56.5 miles south of Shoshone, the last site in the previous chapter. From Baker, take Kelbaker Road to Kelso. The town is also 22.5 miles north of Interstate 40. Take the Amboy-Kelso Exit.*

## Goffs

Goffs, like Kelso (see preceding entry), is another delightful anomaly of the Mojave Desert. Neither town would be in this book if it had not been for the determination of a few individuals to preserve, at each site, a single worthy, historic building. If not for those determined efforts, both Kelso and Goffs would have essentially disappeared.

Goffs came into being in 1883 when the Southern Pacific Railway completed a route between Barstow and Needles. Goffs was at the highest point along that line, a siding at what was called the "Top of the Hill." It grew in importance that same year when a short line, the Nevada Southern Railway, extended north from Goffs.

The origin of the town's name is a little uncertain, although the stops along the Southern Pacific from Amboy, which is west of Goffs, started a sequence of alphabetical watering stations that proceeded east to the Arizona border: Amboy, Bristol, Cadiz, Danby, Edson (later Essex), Fenner, and Goffs. According to Erwin Gudde, author of *California Place Names*, all but the first of these names came from other towns of the same names elsewhere in the United States. He also says that apparently there were members of the Amboy family in the Southern Pacific organization to account for the first name.

Goffs grew sufficiently to warrant a school in 1911, with classes held in a rented building. The present schoolhouse, erected in 1914, served the town well as school, community center, and branch library.

In 1926, an old wagon road became a part of the National Old Trails Road, which then became legendary Route 66. Only five years later, however, Route 66 was altered to eliminate Goffs, and the town began its decline. The school closed in 1937, and when U.S. troops were stationed in the Goffs area for desert training during World War II, services were so sparse in the town that the schoolhouse was used as a cafe.

When I first saw the Goffs Schoolhouse in the early 1980s, it was in such disrepair that I didn't think it could be saved. How mistaken I was. Dennis and Jo Ann Casebier bought the property in 1990, and the resurrection began, culminating in the building's placement on the National Register of Historic Places.

On your way to Goffs, you drive for more than ten miles along the original Route 66, now a secondary road with its share of potholes, seeing

The Goffs Schoolhouse, erected in 1914, served the town as a community center and library as well. Note the original concrete fencepost in the foreground.

virtually no sign of civilization other than the Burlington Northern Santa Fe Railway tracks that accompany you. Then, emerging from the desert landscape, stands the unusual Goffs Schoolhouse, which now serves as a museum that features informative displays, extensive mining and railroad equipment, and various other artifacts. Along with the authentic school is a reconstruction of the Goffs depot, used as a library with a comprehensive collection of books on the Mojave Desert. A small cemetery with seven apparent graves stands nearby.

To visit Goffs from Kelso, head south on Kelbaker Road for 22.5 miles to Interstate 40. From there, drive 28.6 miles east to the Fenner-Goffs Exit. Fenner has virtually disappeared except for an operating service station. Goffs is 10.9 miles northeast on the paved Goffs Road that is also Historic Route 66.

*Important Note: The Goffs Schoolhouse and Museum is not always open. Visit the Mojave Desert Heritage and Cultural Association website (www.mdhca.org) for more information.*

# CALICO

Calico and Bodie (see page 146) are at the extremes of what the term "ghost town" encompasses. Bodie is in a state of arrested decay, carefully preserved so that we can experience the past. Calico is always changing, an asphalt-lined homage to capitalism that stretches the term "ghost town" to its limit—and perhaps beyond. It begins when you see, from a distance, "CALICO" in large letters, reminiscent of the famous Hollywood sign, on the side of King Mountain. Calico is not the genuine article, but it can be an entertaining family adventure as long as you accept it for what it is—a tourist spot.

When John Peterson heard in 1881 that his friends Hulse Thomas, Tom Warden, George Yager, and G. Frank Mecham were headed to prospect for the next big strike, he said the mountains near their destination were "calico-colored," a name that stuck for the mountain range, a prominent peak, and the eventual town.

The four prospectors did indeed find the next big strike, which they named the Silver King. The claim would produce more silver than any other mine in California during the 1880s. Along with approximately sixty other mines, the Silver King made Calico the greatest of the Southern California silver towns, with an estimated $86 million extricated over a period of fifteen years.

In addition to silver, Calico also had enormous Colemanite borax deposits nearby, and, because the mines were only twelve miles from a rail stop at Daggett, the new discoveries made the Death Valley mines relatively unprofitable by comparison (although plenty of borax still remains there today). Those mines ceased production, causing the death of Ryan (see page 190).

On the other hand, Calico grew to a town of about 1,200 by 1886, featuring a school with around 50 students, a post office, a Wells Fargo office, the usual stores, saloons, gambling parlors, and a red-light district. The local newspaper was a delightful pun: The Calico *Print*.

By 1890, Calico had almost tripled to a population of as many as 3,500 citizens. Most of the buildings were made of adobe, including boardinghouses, restaurants, assay offices, and a shoe-and-boot shop with its own bar.

A mere three years later, in 1893, Calico began its descent from boom to bust. A steady decline in silver prices, due to increased supply and decreased coinage, culminated in the repeal of the Sherman Silver Purchase Act. This act had previously guaranteed acquisition of almost nine million ounces of silver per

Calico's schoolhouse is a replica, built in 1954, of a building that stood on the same location during Calico's heyday.

month by the federal government. Its repeal meant that the coin of the realm was gold—and only gold. The result was the Silver Panic of 1893, and mines all over the country closed. By 1896, Calico's mines began to play out as well: the combination of drastically lower prices for the ore and a diminished supply from the mines spelled the end, and Calico rapidly became a ghost, with many of its buildings moved to nearby communities. A modest rebirth occurred in about 1915 when a cyanide plant was constructed to recover silver that remained in the original waste dumps. One of the workers in that plant was Walter Knott, who, with his wife, Cordelia, was homesteading nearby.

The Knotts subsequently became well known in Southern California for their berry farm (Walter created the boysenberry by crossing the red raspberry, the blackberry, and the loganberry), which evolved into the now-famous Knott's Berry Farm, an Orange County theme park. In 1951, the Knotts purchased Calico and began to restore it; they eventually donated the town to San Bernardino County in 1966, and it is now part of the County of San Bernardino Regional Parks.

Calico's former courthouse served for decades as the residence of Lucy Lane, who became known as the "Queen of Calico." Now a museum, the adobe structure features many artifacts belonging to her. For this photo, the Lane House and most of Calico was dressed up for the Christmas season.

## WALKING AROUND CALICO

Calico contains well over two dozen buildings, many with elaborate falsefronts and gingerbread trim, showcasing what the movies have caused us to expect in an Old West town. The problem is that none of them are authentic. Among those fanciful creations, however, stand a few original buildings, along with one faithful reproduction.

When you enter Calico from the parking lot, the second building on your left will be the Park Office. That's where I found a brochure called "Walking Tour of Old Calico," much preferable to the "Visitor Guide and Map" that is widely distributed in the park. The walking tour will lead you straight to Calico's more genuine articles. Here are the best three of the brochure's nine stops:

The Park Office is an original building, although of unknown date or purpose. It has the look of a residence as opposed to a commercial building.

Lil's Saloon/Drug Store dates from the 1880s. It has been a drug store, the office of a doctor, and a Wells Fargo office. It may have served other purposes as well, perhaps as the site of an ice cream store and a millinery shop. Its last known use was as a museum in the 1940s, when Calico was a true ghost.

The Courthouse/Lane Home is the gem of the old buildings. It is a museum, but, more than that, it is a tribute to Lucy Lane, the "Queen of Calico," who lived in the town for almost sixty-seven years. She came to town as a ten-year-old with her family, saw the boom years, and met and married her husband, John, there. They left a then–ghost town in 1899 but returned for good in 1916. The best room in the building is the Lane Room, originally the home's kitchen, which contains photographs of Lucy and John along with many of their possessions.

The Calico Cemetery is one of the rare authentic places in the town. The headstone on the far right with the respectful pair of cowboy boots is for "Tumbleweed" Harris (1906–1979), one of several volunteers or park employees who are buried in the cemetery.

A fourth building worth visiting is a 1955 replica of the schoolhouse, which stands on a hill slightly northwest of the main town. It is located where the original stood, although it is about a third smaller. Be sure to peer inside at the furnishings. Lucy Lane attended classes here in her youth. The last teacher, Margaret Kincaid Olivier, is buried in the Calico Cemetery.

Be sure to stop at that graveyard before you leave the park in your car. It's on a hill to the west as you descend from the townsite. Margaret Olivier's stone marker is on the left about five rows north of the entrance. Several graves are relatively recent, some for volunteers who gave their time as greeters, docents, and, in one case, as "sheriff."

If you are a purist, and you love the solitude and isolation that ghost town hunting often brings, then I'd say you may want to skip Calico. It is the only site in the three chapters on central and Southern California that totally lacks that elusive "ghost town feeling." If you have children along, however, I think they'd enjoy it.

Incidentally, on my last visit I must have seen fifteen cats wandering around town. None was a calico.

## WHEN YOU GO

*From Kelso, drive 22.5 miles south on Kelbaker Road to I-40. Take I-40 west for 80 miles to Barstow. From downtown Barstow, head northeast on Interstate 15 for 6.7 miles, getting off at Exit 191, Ghost Town Road. Calico is 3.9 miles north with the way clearly marked.*

# RANDSBURG

Most of the historical accounts in this book are about men, simply because most of the towns included here were settled early on by an almost entirely male population. In addition, the heads of mining companies were traditionally male, as were the leaders of expeditions. If you are looking for a story of a strong-willed, intelligent, highly educated woman who was prominent in her town's history and success, you have found it.

Dr. Rose Burcham's husband, Charles Austin Burcham, had a bad case of gold fever. To appease it, Dr. Burcham, a respected general practitioner in San Bernardino, had grubstaked her husband for two years' worth of prospecting in the desert. The time had almost expired when Charles and his fellow adventurers John Singleton and Frederic Mooers made claims near Goler Wash in April 1895. In a clever ruse, the three filled a wagon full of their "find" and visited a nearby camp. Miners there peered under the tarp, saw worthless quartz, and dismissed the three prospectors as ignorant fools. What they did not realize was that the "fools" knew perfectly well that their load was worthless—nor did they realize that the real ore of their claims would yield a true bonanza—the Rand Mine.

The mine was named in hopeful emulation of a huge gold strike in South Africa, Witwatersrand (commonly known as the Rand). The town that grew up around the California mine was originally Rand Camp, later Randsburg. The name of the mine itself became the Yellow Aster, the title of a book Mooers had been reading.

Charles Burcham and his male partners were almost immediately offered quick money to sell the claims; fortunately, there was a fourth partner. Rose Burcham insisted that the four retain total control of the mine, refusing all outside capital. This was a woman who had already broken barriers, practicing medicine in a virtually entirely male profession. Many a potential investor walked away from the Yellow Aster muttering about "that woman," but her intransigence paid off. They all became millionaires.

Randsburg grew as the Yellow Aster prospered. In the summer of 1896, only a little more than a year after the discovery, the camp had a population of about a thousand. Within three years, the population more than tripled.

By 1899 the Yellow Aster had a payroll exceeding $13,000 per month, paid to a hundred and fifty workers. A one-hundred-stamp mill processed the ore. Dr. Burcham, who in the earliest days kept the books and cooked the

Randsburg's Butte Street contains several of the best ghost town buildings in Southern California. Here you see the General Store, the adobe former post office, and the former union hall with its corrugated falsefront.

meals, became the dominant partner. Marcia Rittenhouse Wynn, who grew up in Randsburg and wrote about the early days, described Dr. Burcham as a "brilliant, business-like, crisp, hard-working, exacting person." Her presence was felt in every detail of the operation: for example, the Yellow Aster's stamp mill—usually a dark and dingy place—was kept spotless, with a potted palm residing in the main engine room.

Within five years of the discovery of the Yellow Aster, an estimated $3 million had been taken from the district's mines, the largest amount from the Yellow Aster itself.

Because it was primarily a company town, Randsburg was hardly the raucous place some mining towns were. It was spirited, but not rowdy, and its small jail had only two cells. But Randsburg was the site of union strife. When an attempt was made to make the Yellow Aster a fully unionized mine, a strike resulted that lasted from 1902 until 1916. Production continued, however, with nonunion miners. The town was divided in its sympathies: on Saturday nights, two dances were held, union and nonunion, and girls who were observed at one dance were not welcome at the other.

The Rand District's mines produced on a large scale until 1918, with an estimated total of $20 million, $12 million of which came directly from the Yellow Aster. In addition to gold, smaller amounts of silver and tungsten were also extracted. Smaller-scale mining continued into the 1930s and 1940s, and no doubt someone is still digging in those hills. The Rand District was the largest producer of gold ore in Southern California.

The Randsburg City Jail is a stout and incommodious building. Imagine occupying one of the two cells in the Mojave Desert's summer heat.

## WALKING AND DRIVING AROUND RANDSBURG

If you are coming from Calico, the previous entry in this chapter, you will enter Randsburg from the north. As the main road takes a bend, you will see the stark, two-cell jail on your left. Read the historical plaque and then take a look inside. At this writing the jail has two unfortunate mannequin inhabitants, an obvious Lady of the Evening and an over-imbiber wearing a red shirt, very likely a member of E Clampus Vitus (for more on that society, see the Murphys entry, page 48). I determined that he is a Clamper both by his shirt (Clampers wear red shirts at all their activities) and by his empty whiskey bottle—*especially* by the empty bottle. You are invited to toss coins into the cells to help them "raise bail." I threw a quarter into the lady's cell and then gazed at the other miscreant. As a fellow Clamper, I winced at his sorry condition. So I threw in a second quarter—into the lady's cell. That Clamper is going to have to extricate himself.

Now continue south into the heart of Randsburg, where you will see some of the finest historic buildings in central or Southern California. In the middle of three of the best along Butte Street is what once served as the post office, made of adobe to withstand fires. Adjacent to the post office on the right is the corrugated falsefront of the former union hall, headquarters for the union movement during the labor troubles. It also served for a time as the post office. On the left of the adobe building is the town's general store, now the hub of activity in Randsburg. Three other false-front commercial buildings are adjacent to these first three.

Across the street is the White House Saloon, which features a long bar created to accommodate thirsty miners. A door in the basement of the saloon once opened into a tunnel that led toward the Yellow Aster Mine. Local lore says that it was used occasionally for high-grading the mine. Several other businesses make

Randsburg's White House Saloon, still very much in operation, is rumored to have had a tunnel that led toward the Yellow Aster Mine, perhaps to aid in the highgrading of ore.

up the remainder of the Butte Street area, as well as the informative Randsburg Desert Museum (open on Saturday, Sunday, and holidays), which features a display of mining equipment, including a five-stamp mill.

Continue east on Butte until it intersects Lexington. On the northeast corner stands the board-and-batten 1904 Santa Barbara Catholic Church. Take Lexington around to the west to see a series of residences and the 1934–35 Community Methodist Episcopal Church.

The Yellow Aster Mine, which was the original reason for the Rand District excitement, stands on a hill south of town and is closed to the public.

In addition to Randsburg, several lesser sites make up the Rand District. East of Randsburg is Johannesburg, whose primary historic remnant is its cemetery, which is southwest of the commercial area at Mountain Wells Avenue and Ophir Street. Directly behind the graveyard is the King Solomon Mine.

South of Johannesburg 1.5 miles on U.S. Highway 395 is Red Mountain, whose historic school has been restored as a senior center. Atolia is 2.9 miles south of Red Mountain. Scattered mining debris marks the site. You will pass all of these as you head north from Barstow.

## WHEN YOU GO

*Randsburg is 63.6 miles northwest of Barstow (the town closest to Calico, the previous entry in this chapter). When you leave Johannesburg, at 61.5 miles from Barstow, turn left off U.S. Highway 395 in one mile and take the Redrock-Randsburg Road for 1.1 miles into Randsburg. Signs clearly show the turnoff.*

# THE TROPICO GOLD MINE

The great Nevada Comstock Lode was discovered when a kind of blue sludge, which was hampering progress in the pursuit of paltry amounts of gold, was determined to be so rich in sulphurites of silver that it became the largest silver strike in the history of the United States.

The Tropico Gold Mine is rather like the Comstock Lode, albeit on a much smaller scale, and with an even more inauspicious beginning. Ezra Hamilton was the owner of the East Side Pottery Company, which made sewer pipe for the rapidly growing community of Los Angeles. In 1878, he was looking for a fresh supply of the proper potter's clay and found it on a hill, about fifty miles north of Los Angeles, owned by Dr. L. A. Crandall. After removing clay on a lease basis for four years, Hamilton liked the clay quality so much that he purchased the hill from Crandall in 1882 and continued to remove clay until the demand for sewer pipe declined in 1894.

It was then that Hamilton began to look for other uses for the hill of clay. What he found in the clay was gold, and it was evident in sufficient quantities to

Though the Tropico Gold Mine is closed to visitors at this writing, it remains a photogenic gem.

open a mine, the Lida. One needs to pause at this point to wonder how much gold was caked into the sewers of Los Angeles!

By 1896 the Lida was a solid producer, and in 1908 Hamilton sold the Lida to the Tropico Mining and Milling Company, named for the group of investors who lived in Tropico, a section of Glendale, east of Los Angeles. The mine continued to bring in solid returns until it closed during World War I.

The Tropico reopened in the 1930s when the price of gold was raised by the federal government from $20 to $35 per ounce, but it closed yet again due to World War II with the Gold Limitation Order L-280, which prohibited mining of metals not considered strategic for the war effort. Although some mining was done after the war, the results were minimal. Estimates of total gold production for the lifetime of the mine are between $6 million and $8 million.

The Tropico Gold Mine became a tourist attraction in the late 1950s. I toured the property, which included historic buildings brought to the site, in the mid-1980s. The tour featured excellent historic photos, a large collection of memorabilia, and a view down the main shaft, which is nine hundred feet deep. But at this writing the property is closed to the public and posted against trespassing. The structures at the foot of the mine's hill are deteriorating badly. The name of the mine lives on at a nearby subdivision and at the Tropico Middle School, a part of the Southern Kern Unified School District.

The mine site remains, however, a genuinely photogenic place, which is why you're going to want to visit it and neighboring Willow Springs (see following entry) as you travel from Randsburg down to Llano (see page 224), one of the most unusual sites in this book.

## WHEN YOU GO

*From Randsburg, drive west for 20.5 miles on Redrock-Randsburg Road, where it will join California Highway 14 heading to Mojave, 24 miles southwest. From Mojave, drive 13.8 miles south on California Highway 14 to Rosamond. Exit on Rosamond Boulevard. Drive west for 2.8 miles on Rosamond Boulevard and turn right on Mojave-Tropico Road. Proceed north for 0.8 miles to the closed gate of the Tropico Gold Mine.*

# WILLOW SPRINGS

When Ezra Hamilton's Lida Mine (see Tropico, preceding entry) proved to contain solid, lasting gold deposits, Hamilton purchased a former stage stop at nearby Willow Springs in 1900 to ensure a consistent supply of water to his mine and mill. Entrepreneur that Hamilton was, he also envisioned another use for the reliable source of water: he constructed a resort for sufferers of lung diseases, offering a shady oasis in the dry desert air. Built at a cost of $40,000, the complex, which opened in 1904, consisted of twenty-seven buildings, including residences, a hotel, a store with a post office, a garage, a power plant, an icehouse, a school, a community center, a dance hall, a bathhouse, and a swimming pool. The grounds were planted with mulberry trees, an orchard, and vineyards. The resort operated until a few years after Hamilton's death in 1914, the post office closed in 1918, and the school became part of the Rosamond district in the late 1920s.

The dependable supply of water at Willow Springs had been used long before Ezra Hamilton. The first human users of the desert springs were likely indigenous Native Americans, followed by the Padre Garces–led Spanish in 1776. Garces was a Franciscan missionary who explored Southern California extensively. John C. Frémont, who became legendary as the Pathfinder of the West, stopped there with an exploration party in 1844, only twelve years before he became the Republican Party's candidate for President of the United States.

The Willow Springs Dance Hall and Saloon even features swinging doors (on the left), although they appear to be of modern origin.

In 1849, the Jayhawker Party, having narrowly escaped Death Valley, also stopped at Willow Springs. The site had its busiest times in the 1860s, when freight wagons going to and from Cerro Gordo (see page 166), as well as a stagecoach line that went between Los Angeles and Havilah (now a small town south of Lake Isabella), made Willow Springs a regular stop along their way, stocking up on food and water for travelers, horses, and beasts of burden.

## WALKING AROUND WILLOW SPRINGS

The news about Willow Springs is very good since my first visit in the 1980s. The site—owned by The Willow Springs Company Reserve Systems, Incorporated—is being completely refurbished using authentic materials and methods. On your way into the town from the south, you will see a 1937 California Historical Landmark plaque on the left side of the road next to a large concrete trough. By my count there are ten one-story buildings, three of adobe and seven of rock. People working at the site were very friendly and invited me to take a look around, a pleasant change from some privately owned historic sites. A vineyard has been installed just north of the main buildings, with the vines carefully arranged so they do not encroach on a deserted residence that is due for restoration. The first building you will come to on your left has faded letters spelling "garage" across its metal doors, along with a gravity-fed gas pump. The former dance hall is next door; across the street stands an occupied residence along with several other structures. A second, more recent California Historical Landmark plaque is located next to the road in the center of the complex.

A roofless stone ruin stands east of the Tehachapi-Willow Springs Road north of the turnoff that you took onto Truman Road.

## WHEN YOU GO

*Willow Springs is 5.3 miles from the Tropico Gold Mine. From that mine's locked gate, return south to Rosamond Boulevard and turn right (west). In 3.5 miles, turn north on Tehachapi-Willow Springs Road (also signed as 90th Street West). Turn west on Truman Road in 0.7 of a mile and turn right on Manley Road to enter Willow Springs in 0.3 of a mile.*

# LLANO

Llano is one of the very best sites I know for the true ghost town purist, and that's why it's in this book. The purist doesn't need, or expect, swinging doors in the vacant saloon. In fact, some of his or her best experiences have occurred where a casual observer might say, "I don't see a thing."

On a stretch of the Pearblossom Highway east of Palmdale stands a place where hundreds, probably thousands, of cars zoom past daily, their drivers not knowing or caring that they are passing through a dream that was born and died right there, out in the Mojave Desert. The true ghost town enthusiast lives for such places. I have visited and catalogued more than six hundred ghost towns, and nothing is quite like Llano.

The first settlement of Llano (Spanish for "level field," "plain," or "even ground" and pronounced "*yah*-no") occurred in about 1888, perhaps by Quakers. A post office was established in 1890, and by 1895 a community of about a hundred people featured a school, the post office (that by then also had a store), and a nearby doctor. The town was dead in a mere five years because the Big Rock Creek Irrigation Project, which was to provide the town with water for crops, failed. The post office closed in 1900.

The second Llano, whose remnants you will be exploring, came to life in 1914 when a Los Angeles lawyer and prominent socialist, Job Harriman, acquired the land. Harriman wanted to prove that the socialist theory of cooperative living could thrive in a desert utopia.

To participate in the colony, members purchased shares and were paid a sum of $4.00 per day for whatever work they were assigned to do. The payments were, however, on paper, not cash. The first building erected was a 7,500-square-foot hotel, which housed visitors as well as colony bachelors. The structure also featured a barbershop, a library, a printing shop, and an assembly/dining hall with two large stone fireplaces.

At its peak between 1915 and 1917, Llano was a busy, if not thriving, community of about nine hundred citizens, making it the largest town by far in the Antelope Valley. Almost 2,000 acres were being cultivated, but the land wasn't all that productive. At one point the colonists' diet consisted primarily of carrots.

In addition to being farmers, the members worked in a dairy, a cannery, a rug-making factory, a steam laundry, a cleaning-pressing-dyeing plant, and a soap-making factory. The colony's printing shop published a weekly newspaper, the *Llano Colonist* as well as a monthly magazine, the *Western Comrade*. Children

These stone and concrete ruins are what is left of the 7,500-square-foot of Llano's combination hotel/dining room/meeting hall/barbershop/printing shop/library, which also housed the colony's bachelors.

attended the colony's school, and social activities included swimming, music, riflery, team sports, and weekly dances.

Lack of water, which caused the demise of the original Llano, became central to the failure of the second. Despite elaborate rock-lined ditches constructed to tap the water of Big Rock Creek, insufficient water was a constant problem. A second problem came from within the very nature of the colonists. According to former member Tony Vacik, "Some people just will not cooperate. Fourteen comrades would be assigned to a project and probably four of them would do all the work." Equal payment for unequal effort had its drawbacks.

Discouraged by the prospects of the Llano del Rio Cooperative Colony, Harriman and other leaders decided to try again in Louisiana, purchasing 20,000 acres there and calling it Newllano. The Antelope Valley site was abandoned, and the new Louisiana colony fared little better than the first. Harriman soon returned to Los Angeles and died there in 1925 at the age of sixty-four.

## WALKING AND DRIVING AROUND LLANO

I first learned about Llano in 1982 from a 1963 article in *Desert Magazine*. I expected little would be left, especially considering the population explosion that had taken place in California during those nearly twenty years. A friend living in Palmdale, who routinely drove the Pearblossom Highway, confirmed my expectations. He assured me that no ghost town was there; however, I decided to take a look for myself in August of 1982.

And there it was, to my amazement, virtually unchanged from the photos in the magazine. I returned again almost thirty years later, in 2010, believing that this time it really *must* have vanished under a developer's bulldozer. Imagine my delight to find it still unchanged. It was like visiting a seemingly ageless old friend.

Many of the buildings and water ditches in Llano used lime from two kilns. This one is southeast of the colony on Bobs Gap Road.

Your best point of reference for exploring Llano is the intersection of California Highway 138 and 165th Street. East of that intersection on the north side of the highway stand four stone pillars and two fifteen-foot stone chimneys that delineate the hotel/dining room/meeting hall. If you walk around, you'll notice near the ruin the remnants of the lined ditches that carried water to the irrigated fields. North of the hotel are long rock walls of the horse barn and two foundations.

You can either walk or drive to the largest remnants. Visible from the hotel on the south side of the highway is a tall (about thirty feet in height) concrete silo. You can reach it by going straight toward it on any one of several tracks, or you can return to 165th Street and drive south for 0.5 of a mile. There you'll find a road going east that at this writing has a "no dumping" sign (that has been, unfortunately, largely ignored). Before driving in, look west across 165th Street. You will see the concrete foundation of the colony's school. When you head east and reach the silo, you'll also see the long, stout rock walls of the dairy barn.

Two more colony structures remain. Return to 165th Street and head south. It becomes Bob's Gap Road. When the highway turns toward the southeast, continue south on the dirt road into Rancho de la Vista, which at this writing has a sign saying it's a private road but does not say "no trespassing." I've had residents give me a friendly

The easiest structure in Llano to spot from the highway is a large concrete silo next to the former dairy barn.

wave, so I don't think driving in is any problem. From the entrance to Rancho de la Vista, continue south for one mile and then head east on Avenue Y-8. In 0.3 of a mile, on a hill to the north about 200 yards from Y-8, you can see a stone limekiln.

To see the final remnant of Llano del Rio Cooperative Colony, return to Bob's Gap Road and turn right (southeast). Continue 2.1 miles toward Bob's Gap, a dramatic natural cut in Holcomb Ridge. Near the end of the gap, tucked into a wall on the northeast side of the road, stands a second limekiln, more elaborate than the first. Adjacent to it is a roofless ruin. The kilns produced the lime that was used in the mortar for all those rock and stone buildings you have visited, as well as for the ditches that, they hoped, would bring much-needed water to the colony.

When you return toward the Pearblossom Highway, note the ultimate irony: the utopian desert dream town died largely because of the hardships caused by a lack of water. Now millions of gallons of it pass across the southern border of the colony along the giant California Aqueduct.

## WHEN YOU GO

*From Rosamond (the town nearest the Tropico Gold Mine and Willow Springs), drive 20.2 miles south on California Highway 14 to Palmdale. Llano is 20 miles east of Palmdale on the Pearblossom Highway (California Highway 138) and 4.5 miles east of the small community of Pearblossom. For more specific directions, consult "Walking and Driving Around Llano," above.*

# ACKNOWLEDGMENTS

For assistance in historical research: Buzz Baxter, Chinese Camp, California; Elizabeth Braydis, Calaveras Historical Society, California; Dennis Casebier, Goffs, California; Robert Desmarais, Cerro Gordo, California; Shirley Harding, Death Valley, California; Merv Hoffman, Kennedy Mine Tour, Jackson, California; Ross Hopkins, Death Valley, California; Virginia Lutes, Kentucky Mine, Sierra City, California; Mike Meadows, Ryan, California; Judy Palmer, Shoshone, California; Jody Stewart Patterson and Mike Patterson, Cerro Gordo, California; Mike Rauschkolb, Ryan, California; George Ross, Shoshone, California; Bill Schreier, Death Valley, California; Matthew S. Sugarman, Marshall Gold Discovery State Historic Park, Coloma, California.

For field-work support: Diane Holland, Auburn, California; and Warren and Mary Weaver, La Cañada, California.

For photographic and technical assistance: Mike Moore, Elgin, Arizona; and John Scott, Tucson, Arizona.

And, perhaps most importantly, for navigation and company on the back roads, grateful thanks to trip companions Warren Weaver; MaryAnn Mead; Mike Moore; and my daughter, Janet Varney.

# GLOSSARY OF MINING TERMS

**adit**: A nearly horizontal entrance to a hard-rock mine.

**Argonaut**: A man who came to California during the Gold Rush (after the Argonauts of Greek mythology who sailed on the ship *Argo* in search of riches).

**arrastra**: An apparatus used to grind ore by means of a heavy stone that is dragged around in a circle, normally by mules or oxen.

**assay**: To determine the value of a sample of ore, in ounces per ton, by testing using a chemical evaluation.

**bonanza**: To miners, a body of rich ore.

**charcoal kiln** (or oven): A structure into which wood is placed and subjected to intense heat through a controlled, slow burning. Charcoal is a longer-lasting, more efficient wood fuel often used to power mills and smelters. If the kiln is used to convert coal to coke, it's called a coke oven.

**chloride**: Usually refers to ores containing chloride of silver.

**claim**: A tract of land with defined boundaries that includes mineral rights extending downward from the surface.

**claim-jumping (or jumping a claim)**: Illegally taking over someone else's claim.

**diggings (or diggins)**: Evidence of mining efforts, such as placer, hydraulic, or dredge workings.

**dredge**: An apparatus, usually on a flat-bottomed boat, that scoops material out of a river to extract gold-bearing sand or gravel; used in "dredging" or "dredge mining."

**dust**: Minute gold particles found in placer deposits.

**flotation**: A method of mineral separation in a mill in which water, in combination with chemicals, "floats" finely crushed minerals of value to separate them from the detritus, which sinks. Process used in a flotation mill.

**flume**: An inclined, man-made channel, usually of wood, used to convey water or mine waste, often for long distances.

**gallows frame**: See "headframe," below.

**giant**: The nozzle on the end of a pipe through which water is forced in hydraulic mining. Also called a monitor.

**grubstake**: An advance of money, food, and/or supplies to a prospector in return for a share of any discoveries.

**hard-rock mining**: The process in which a "primary deposit" (see below) is mined by removing ore-bearing rock by tunneling into the earth. Also known as quartz mining, since gold is frequently found in quartz deposits.

**headframe**: The vertical apparatus over a mine shaft that has cables to be lowered down the shaft for raising either ore or a cage; sometimes called a "gallows frame."

**high-grade ore**: Rich ore.

**high-grading**: The theft of rich ore, usually by a miner working for someone else who owns the mine.

**hopper**: In mining, a structure with funnels from which the contents, loaded from above, can be emptied for purposes of transportation.

**horn silver**: Silver chloride, a native ore of silver. Also known as Cerargyrite.

**hydraulic mining**: A method of mining using powerful jets of water to wash away a bank of gold-bearing earth. Also known by miners as "hydraulicking."

**ingot**: A cast bar or block of a metal.

**lode**: A continuous mineral-bearing deposit or vein (see also "Mother Lode," below).

**mill**: A building in which rock is crushed to extract minerals by one of several methods. If this is done by stamps (heavy hammers or pestles), it is a stamp mill. If by iron balls, it is a ball mill. The mill is usually constructed on the side of a hill to utilize its slope—hence, a "gravity-fed mill."

**mining district**: An area of land described (usually for legal purposes) and designated as containing valuable minerals in paying amounts.

**monitor**: See "giant," above.

**Mother Lode**: The principal lode passing through a district or section of the country; from the same term in Spanish, "La Veta Madre." In California, it refers specifically to the hundred-mile-long concentration of gold on the western slopes of the Sierra Nevada.

**mucker**: A person or machine that clears material like rock in a mine.

**nugget**: A lump of native gold or other mineral. The largest found in California's Mother Lode weighed 195 pounds.

**ore**: A mineral of sufficient concentration, quantity, and value to be mined at a profit.

**ore sorter**: A structure, usually near a mine, in which higher-grade ore is sorted from lower-grade ore or waste before being sent to the mill or smelter.

**pan**: To look for placer gold by washing earth, gravel, or sand, usually in a streambed, by using a shallow, concave dish called a "pan."

**placer**: A waterborne deposit of sand or gravel containing heavier materials like gold, which have been eroded from their original bedrock and concentrated as small particles that can be washed, or "panned," out (see also "secondary deposit," below).

**pocket**: In primary deposits, a small but rich concentration of gold embedded in quartz. In secondary deposits, a hole or indentation in a streambed in which gold dust or nuggets have been trapped.

**powderhouse**: A structure placed safely away from a mine that stored such volatile materials as gun powder or dynamite. The building's walls are usually very stout, but its roof is intentionally of flimsier construction, so if the contents should explode, the main force of the blast would be into the air.

**primary deposit**: A deposit of gold or other mineral found in its original location. Ore is extracted by hard-rock mining, or hydraulic mining.

**prospect**: Mineral workings of unproven value.

**prospector**: He who searches for prospects.

**quartz mining**: See "hard-rock mining."

**rocker**: A portable "sluicebox" used by prospectors.

**salting**: To place valuable minerals in a place in which they do not actually occur. Done to deceive. Therefore, a salted claim is one that is intended to lure the unsuspecting investor into a scam.

**secondary deposit**: A deposit of gold or other mineral that has moved from its original location by water. Ore is extracted by placer mining or dredging.

**shaft**: A vertical or nearly vertical opening into the earth for hard-rock mining.

**slag**: The waste product of a smelter; hence, "slag dumps."

**sluicebox**: A wooden trough in which placer deposits are sluiced, or washed, to retrieve gold from the deposits.

**smelter**: A building or complex in which material is melted in order to separate impurities from pure metal.

**square set**: A set of timbers that are cut so that they form a ninety-degree angle and so that they can be combined with other "sets" to create a framework that safely buttresses a mine. First used in Nevada's Comstock Lode.

**strike**: The discovery of a primary or secondary deposit of gold or other mineral in sufficient concentration and/or quantity to be mined profitably.

**tailings:** Waste or refuse left after milling is complete; sometimes used more generally, although incorrectly, to indicate waste dumps. Because of improved technology, older tailings have often been reworked to extract minerals that were left behind from an older, cruder, milling process.

**tramway**: An apparatus for moving materials such as ore, rock, or even supplies in buckets suspended from pulleys that run on a cable.

**tunnel**: A horizontal or nearly horizontal underground passage open at one end at least.

**vein**: A zone or belt of valuable mineral within less valuable neighboring rock.

**waste dump**: Waste rock, not of sufficient value to warrant milling, that comes out of the mine; usually found immediately outside the mine entrance.

**workings**: A general term indicating any mining development; when that development is exhausted, it is "worked out."

# BIBLIOGRAPHY

Alotta, Robert I. *Signposts and Settlers: The History of Place Names West of the Rockies.* Chicago: Bonus Books, 1994.

*American West.* The. may/June 1976.

Bailey, Lynn R. *Supplying the Mining World.* Tucson, AZ: Westernlore Press, 1996.

Beck, Warren A., and Ynez D. Haase. *Historical Atlas of California.* Norman, OK: University of Oklahoma Press, 1974.

Billeb, Emil W. *Mining Camp Days.* Las Vegas: Nevada Publications, 1968.

*Branding Iron.* No 183, Spring 1991.

Brewer, William H. *Up and Down California.* New Haven, CT: Yale University Press, 1974.

Bruff, Joseph Goldsborough. *Gold Rush.* New York: Columbia University Press, 1949.

Burton, Jeffery F., Mary M. Farrell, Florence B. Lord, and Richard W. Lord. *Confinement and Ethnicity: An Overview of World War II Japanese American Relocation Sites.* Tucson, AZ: Western Archeological and Conservation Center (National Park Service, Department of the Interior), 1999.

Cain, Ella M. *The Story of Bodie.* San Francisco: Fearon Publishers, 1956.

*California Geology.* February 1982; April 1982; June 1982; November 1982; March 1983; May 1983; March 1984; March 1987.

*California Historical Landmarks.* Sacramento: Department of Recreation, State of California, 1979, rev. 1981.

*California Historical Quarterly.* Vols. 14, 26, 54, 56, 66, 67.

Carter, William. *Ghost Towns of the West.* Menlo Park, CA: Lane Magazine and Book Company, 1971 and 1978.

Casebier, Dennis G. *Goffs and Its Schoolhouse.* Essex, CA: Tales of the Mojave Road Publishing Company, 1995.

Caughey, John. *Gold Is the Cornerstone.* Berkeley, CA: University of California Press, 1948.

Chalfant, W.A. *Death Valley: The Facts.* Stanford, CA: Stanford University Press, 1930.

———. *Gold, Guns and Ghost Towns.* Stanford, CA: Stanford University Press, 1947.

———. *The Story of Inyo.* Chicago: Hammond Press, 1922.

Chidsey, D. B. *The California Gold Rush.* New York: Crown Publishers, 1968.

Clark, Lew, and Ginny Clark. *High Mountains and Deep Valleys: The Gold Bonanza Days.* San Luis Obispo, CA: Western Trails Publications, 1978.

*Death Valley: A Guide.* Federal Writers' Project of the Works Progress Administration. Boston: Houghton Mifflin, 1939.

*Desert Magazine.* June 1958; December 1959; April 1961; May 1961; June 1961; September 1961; July 1962; February 1963; May 1963; May 1964.

Dillon, Richard H. *Exploring the Mother Lode Country.* Pasadena, CA: Ward Ritchie Press, 1974.

*Discovering Locke,* n.d.

Florin, Lambert. *California Ghost Towns.* Seattle: Superior Publishing Co., 1871.

Forward, Charles N. (editor). *British Columbia: Its Resources and People.* Victoria, BC, Canada: University of Victoria, 1987.

Gillenkirk, Jeff, and James Motlow. *Bitter Melon.* Berkeley CA: Heyday Books, 1987.

*Gold Rush Country.* Menlo Park, CA: Lane Books, 1968.

Gudde, Erwin G. *California Gold Camps*. Berkeley, CA: University of California Press, 1975.

———. *California Place Names*, 3rd ed. Berkeley, CA: University of California Press, 1969.

Hensher, Alan, and Jack Peskin. *Ghost Towns of the Kern and Eastern Sierra: A Concise Guide.* Los Angeles: private printing, 1980.

Hensher, Alan, and Larry Vredenburgh. *Ghost Towns of the Upper Mojave Desert*, 3rd ed. Los Angeles: private printing, 1987.

Hill, Mary. *Gold: The California Story*. Berkeley, CA: University of California Press, 1999.

Holliday, J. S. *The World Rushed In*. New York: Simon & Schuster, 1981.

Hoover, Mildred Brooke, Hero Eugene Rensch, Ethel Grace Rensch, and William N. Abeloe (revised by Douglas E. Kyle). *Historic Spots in California*, 4th ed. Stanford, CA.: Stanford University Press, 1990.

Hubbard, Douglass. *Ghost Mines of Yosemite*. Fresno, CA: Awani Press, 1971.

Hulbert, Archer Butler. *Forty-Niners: The Chronicle of the California Trail*. Boston: Little, Brown, 1931.

Jackson, Joseph Henry. *Anybody's Gold: The Story of California's Mining Towns*. San Francisco: Chronicle Books, 1970.

——— (editor). *Gold Rush Album*. New York: Charles Scribner's Sons, 1949.

Jenkins, Olaf P. (director). *Geologic Guidebook Along Highway 49– Sierran Gold Belt: The Mother Lode Country*. San Francisco: State of California, Division of Mines, 1948.

Kirk, Ruth. *Exploring Death Valley*. Stanford, CA.: Stanford University Press, 1956.

Leadabrand, Russ. *Exploring California Byways*, vol. V. Los Angeles: Ward Ritchie Press, 1971.

———. *Guidebook to the Mojave Desert of California*. Los Angeles: Ward Ritchie Press, 1966.

Likes, Robert C., and Glenn R. Day. *From This Mountain: Cerro Gordo*. Bishop, CA: Chalfant Press, 1975.

Lingenfelter, Richard. *Death Valley and the Amargosa: A Land of Illusion*. Berkeley, CA: University of California Press, 1986.

Miller, Dean. *Mines of the High Desert*. Glendale, CA: La Siesta Press, 1968.

Miller, Donald. *Ghost Towns of California*. Boulder, CO: Pruett, 1978.

*Mother Lode, The*. Los Angeles: Automobile Club of Southern California, 1982 and 1983 editions.

Moore, Thomas. *Bodie: Ghost Town*. South Brunswick and New York: A. S. Barnes, 1969.

Muir, John. *The Mountains of California*. Berkeley, CA: Ten Speed Press, 1977 (reprint of 1898 edition).

Murbarger, Nell. *Ghosts of the Glory Trail*. Los Angeles: Westernlore Press, 1956.

Murphy, Robert J. *Wildrose Charcoal Kilns*. Bishop, CA: Chalfant Press, 1972.

Myrick, David F. *The Northern Roads: Railroads of Nevada and Eastern California*, vol. 1. Berkeley, CA: Howell-North Books, 1962.

———. *The Southern Roads: Railroads of Nevada and Eastern California*, vol. 2 Berkeley, CA: Howell-North Books, 1963.

Nadeau, Remi. *Ghost Towns and Mining Camps of California*. Los Angeles: Ward Ritchie Press, 1965.

*Northern California Traveler*. July 1996.

*Old Harmony Borax Works*. San Bernardino, CA: Inland Printing and Engraving Co., 1962 (Prepared from Records of the United States Borax and Chemical Corporation).

Paher, Stanley W. *Death Valley Ghost Towns*. Las Vegas: Nevada Publications, 1976.

Palmer, Judy. "Untitled." *Shoshone Museum Reader*, Spring 2010: n.p.

Palmer, Judy, and Susan Sorrells. "Untitled." *Shoshone Museum Reader,* Spring 2009: n.p.

Paul, Rodman W. *California Gold: The Beginning of Mining in the Far West.* Cambridge, MA.: Harvard University Press, 1947.

———. *The California Gold Discovery.* Georgetown, CA: Talisman Press, 1966.

Rolle, Andrew F. *California, A History.* New York: Crowell, 1998.

Roske, Ralph Joseph. *Everyman's Eden.* New York: MacMillan, 1968.

*San Francisco Chronicle.* 7 April 2000.

*San Francisco Examiner.* 4 August 1996; 11 August 1996.

Sprau, David. "A Day in the Life of the Tonopah and Tidewater Railroad." *In Proceedings: Fifth Death Valley Conference on History and Prehistory,* edited by Jean Johnson. Bishop, CA: Community Printing and Publishing, 1999.

Starry, Roberta Martin. *Exploring the Ghost Town Desert.* Los Angeles: Ward Ritchie Press, 1973.

Varney, Philip. *Ghost Towns of Northern California.* Stillwater, MN: Voyageur Press, 2001.

———. *Southern California's Best Ghost Towns.* Norman, OK: University of Oklahoma Press, 1990.

Watkins, T. H. *California, An Illustrated History.* Palo Alto, CA: American West Publishing Co., 1973.

*Wenatchee Daily World.* April 26, 1939.

Williams, George III. *The Guide to Bodie and Eastern Sierra Historic Sites.* Riverside, CA: Tree By the River Publishing, 1981.

Wolle, Muriel Sibell. *The Bonanza Trail.* Chicago: Swallow Press, 1953.

Wood, Raymund F. (editor). *The Westerners Brand Book, #16.* Los Angeles: The Westerners, Los Angeles Corral, 1982.

Wynn, Marcia Rittenhouse. *Desert Bonanza: The Story of Early Randsburg.* Glendale, CA: Arthur H. Clark, Co., 1963.

# INDEX

238

# ABOUT THE AUTHOR AND PHOTOGRAPHER

**PHILIP VARNEY** is the author of eight ghost town guidebooks, including *Ghost Towns of the Mountain West*, *Arizona's Ghost Towns and Mining Camps*, *Southern California's Best Ghost Towns*, and *New Mexico's Best Ghost Towns*.

Varney visited his first ghost town—Central City, Colorado—at the age of eleven and has been an enthusiast ever since. A former high school English teacher and department chairman, he has toured and photographed more than six hundred ghost towns throughout the American West.

In addition to his ghost town books, Varney has authored a book on bicycle tours of southern Arizona, was a contributing writer for Insight Guide's *Wild West*, and has been a contributor to *Arizona Highways* magazine. *True West* magazine has honored Varney as one of the two "Best Living Photographers of the West."

Philip Varney lives in Tucson, Arizona.